Guide to Basic Information Sources

in

ENGLISH LITERATURE

INFORMATION RESOURCES SERIES

Planning Editor: The Late Bill M. Woods

Guide to Basic Information Sources in

ENGLISH LITERATURE

by
Paul A. Doyle
Professor of English
Nassau Community College
State University of New York

With a Foreword by
Harrison T. Meserole
Professor of English
The Pennsylvania State University

A Halsted Press Book
by Jeffrey Norton Publishers, Inc.

John Wiley & Sons

New York   London   Sydney   Toronto

Library of Congress Cataloging in Publication Data

Doyle, Paul A.

Guide to basic information sources in English literature.

(Information resources series)
Includes index.

1. Bibliography—Bibliography—English literature. 2. English literature—History and criticism—Bibliography. 3. Reference books—English literature—Bibliography. 4. Bibliography—Bibliography—American literature. 5. American literature—History and criticism—Bibliography. 6. Reference books—American literature—Bibliography. I. Title.

Z2011.A1D68 [PR83]   016.01682   75-43260
ISBN 0-470-15011-4

Distributed by Halsted Press Division of John Wiley & Sons

Foreword

Engraved in marble on a familiar building is the sentence, "The Library is a summons to scholarship." This is a noble thought, a truth we do not question. Yet for many a young student, budding scholar, or ambitious citizen planning a research project, a library can be an awesome place, with its stack upon stack of shelves stretching from floor to ceiling and reaching deep into mysterious recesses, bearing their burden of countless volumes containing the records of mankind.

To light the way into those recesses, to give the beginner in the library a sense of direction, is the purpose of this **Guide to Basic Information Sources in English Literature.** Used wisely, it can do just that, for within its pages the inquirer can find the precise source to give him a proper start on whatever aspect of English study he wishes to pursue. Even more: he can find the appropriate checklist, bibliography, annotated compilation, literary history, or specialized handbook to tell him what is in print, who wrote it, when it was published, and where it can be located. Each such source will in turn provide direction to other volumes, and those volumes to still others, until the searcher has broadened, or narrowed, the dimensions of his area of inquiry to whatever degree desired.

From the small public community library to the multimillion volume Library of Congress, the key word is **order.** All library resources are organized, catalogued, and numbered to permit rapid location and ease of consultation. And the heart of the library is its reference collection. This is the collection most used by visitors to the library; it is the collection in which many research projects begin. It is, therefore, the collection into which this **Guide** points the way by listing the key titles which serve as first ports of call for the voyager among books; by organizing these titles into functional groups; and by explaining for each title its principal use for the inquirer.

As a pilot book, this **Guide** must be selective. It must choose from among the hundreds, even thousands, of reference sources those titles that are likely to be of most immediate value for the person who is beginning a research project. For example, there are more than a thousand scholarly journals which regularly publish research essays on English and American literature. This **Guide** can list only fifty, adding to each a brief paragraph of descriptive and critical comment detailing its scope, focus, and particular importance. But the **Guide** does direct the searcher to the **MLA International Bibliography** and the **MHRA Bibliography**, which between them survey all thousand journals in the field. Similarly, there are countless sources for the study of Shakespeare. This **Guide** selects nine of the most important, but includes among these the World Shakespeare Bibliography published annually in **Shakespeare Quarterly** and Gordon Ross Smith's **Classified Shakespeare Bibliography 1936-1958**, which between them provide enough research material for even the most knowledgeable scholar.

The two Latin words **vade mecum** ("go with me") are frequently used to describe any object which is constantly carried and regularly used. The experienced author of this **Guide** has produced an informative yet satisfyingly brief and well-organized **vade mecum** which will be of genuine help to anyone contemplating or entering upon a research project for the first time. Another Latin phrase is equally apt: **Verbum sapienti sat est** ("For a wise person a word is enough!").

Harrison T. Meserole
The Pennsylvania State University

March 15, 1976

Preface

Students of English, from college freshman to advanced researcher, have at their disposal not only the creative works of the writers they study but also countless literary reference sources of all types. Indeed, so extensive and numerous are these tools that a guide is extremely valuable and often indispensable to point out the main highways and principal arteries. Otherwise, one easily becomes lost in a labyrinth of almost unlimited sources.

This guide in intended to direct readers to some of the more vital and helpful material amidst the vast amount of data that increase yearly. It is, of necessity, selective, focusing on fundamental references and stressing the more significant writers and literary trends. No bibliographic listing can include all the meritorious English and American literary materials available, far less all of the applicable materials, and I have, therefore, tried to choose for this listing publications that, through their bibliographies and references, will lead readers to further works. Thus, even though particular items may have been omitted, albeit reluctantly, from this guide, if readers carefully use the materials listed, they will generally find information leading to any other materials they may need.

The approach in this book has been, as is reflected by the Contents, to move from basic, general sources to more specific ones. The most fundamental and highly used, as opposed to the more esoteric sources are listed, along with annotations and commentaries. Special sections are included on nonprint information sources and the most important professional organizations. A list of abbreviations is also given.

It should be noted, however, that there is no section devoted exclusively to poetry, but rather that materials on this genre are placed according to their appropriate periods in history. Thus the Raysor and Houtchens books on Romantic poetry and the Faverty work on the Victorian poets are listed under the Nineteenth Century, while the various explication volumes about poetry are reported in the Explication Checklists chapter. In addition, any applicable cross-references, to poetry or otherwise, are given in the Index.

It should also be noted that, because of the considerable variety and complexity of the subject matter, the arrangement of the entries varies from chapter to chapter. Depending on the type of material, entries are sometimes arranged alphabetically, sometimes chronologically, and sometimes in order of importance.

Finally, I could not have written this book without the inspiration and the inquiring minds of my colleagues as well as of the many students with whom I have come in contact during my more than twenty-five years of teaching bibliographic materials. In addition, I must thank the numerous librarians—at the New York Public Library and at several colleges and universities—whose help over these many years has always been immediate, generous, and rewarding.

P. A. DOYLE

Contents

Common Abbreviations Used in English Studies

AES   Abstracts of English Studies
AL   American Literature
AQ   American Quarterly
AS   American Speech
BA   Books Abroad
BAL   Bibliography of American Literature (Jacob Blanck's)
BB   Bulletin of Bibliography
BNYPL   Bulletin of the New York Public Library
BRD   Book Review Digest
BRI   Book Review Index
CA   Contemporary Authors
CBEL   Cambridge Bibliography of English Literature
CCCC   Conference on College Composition and Communication
CE   College English
CEA   College English Association
CL   Comparative Literature
DA   Dissertation Abstracts
DAB   Dictionary of American Biography
DAI   Dissertation Abstracts International
DNB   Dictionary of National Biography
EETS   Early English Text Society
EIC   Essays in Criticism
ELH   ELH [A Journal of English Literary History]
ELN   English Language Notes
ELT   English Literature in Transition, 1880-1920
JEGP   Journal of English and Germanic Philology
KR   Kenyon Review
KSJ   Keats-Shelley Journal
LHUS   Literary History of the United States
MD   Modern Drama
MFS   Modern Fiction Studies
MHRA   Modern Humanities Research Association

MLA	Modern Language Association
MLN	Modern Language Notes
MLQ	Modern Language Quarterly
MLR	Modern Language Review
MP	Modern Philology
NCBEL	New Cambridge Bibliography of English Literature
NCF	Nineteenth Century Fiction
NCTE	National Council of Teachers of English
NED	New English Dictionary
	also known as the
OED	Oxford English Dictionary
N&Q	Notes and Queries
NUC	National Union Catalog
PBSA	Papers of the Bibliographical Society of America
PLL	Papers on Language and Literature
PMLA	Publications of the Modern Language Association of America
PQ	Philological Quarterly
PR	Partisan Review
RES	Review of English Studies
SAQ	South Atlantic Quarterly
SB	Studies in Bibliography
SCN	Seventeenth-Century News
SEL	Studies in English Literature, 1500-1900
SP	Studies in Philology
SQ	Shakespeare Quarterly
SR	Sewanee Review
TCL	Twentieth Century Literature
TEAS	Twayne's English Authors Series
TLS	[London] Times Literary Supplement
TSLL	Texas Studies in Language and Literature
TUSAS	Twayne's United States Authors Series
VQR	Virginia Quarterly Review
VS	Victorian Studies
WHR	Western Humanities Review
YR	Yale Review
YWES	The Year's Work in English Studies

For additional abbreviations, consult the Master List and Table of Abbreviations at the beginning of the MLA International Bibliography.

OTHER ABBREVIATIONS IN THE FIELD

AAAL	American Academy of Arts and Letters
AAUP	American Association of University Professors
abr	abridged
ACE	American Council on Education
ACLS	American Council of Learned Societies
ALA	American Library Association
APA	American Philological Association
enl	enlarged
FR	folio recto (R, on the front of the page)
FV	folio verso (L, on the back of the page)
LC	Library of Congress
LHD	doctor of humanities
LittB	bachelor of letters, bachelor of literature (also BLitt, BLit)
LittD	doctor of letters, doctor of literature (also DLitt, DLit)
ND,n.d.	no date
NEA	National Education Association of the United States
NT	New Testament
OT	Old Testament
PEN	International Association of Poets, Playwrights, Editors, Essayists and Novelists
rev	revised
RSV	Revised Standard Version [of the Bible]
YB	yearbook

Note to The Beginning Researcher

When people are seriously interested in a subject and need more information about it than they have, in many cases they head for a library. Often, however, at the doorway of a good-sized library, confusion sets in owing to uncertainty about how best to use the library's resources. The purpose of this chapter, therefore, is to provide basic information to the beginning researcher on how to get the most out of time spent in the library.

This guide is intended primarily for English students and researchers. It is a source book of information about the subject of English literature, and in particular about how to find this information in the reference room once those at the reference desk have been queried and the card catalog consulted. In this introductory chapter to research, which applies to any beginning researcher, we will mention first the reference desk librarian, then the card catalog, and finally the reference room. At the end of the chapter there is a final note about the arrangement of this book.

THE LIBRARIAN

First, it is a good idea to make use of the knowledge and expertise of the reference librarian. This librarian is often specially trained in the specific discipline you are interested in and may well turn out to be not only your guide at the beginning of your library work, but also, and in general, your most helpful resource. Calling his or her attention to the subject you are researching may well bring suggestions, new ideas or approaches, and other unexpected bonuses. As an example of the last mentioned, many pamphlets, circulars, and other materials are not listed in the card catalog but are kept in file cabinets or on shelves behind the reference desk.

THE CARD CATALOG

Once oriented, most researchers first head for, or are directed to, their first major tool—the card catalog, that modest to imposingly large collection of file drawers that contain arrays of several thousand or even millions of 3 x 5 cards. This catalog contains on its cards an alphabetical listing of all the publications in that library. All books are listed, or indexed, by the author's name. Usually, too, they are indexed by title and under the subject they cover.

Thus, a book such as Richard D. Altick's **The Art of Literary Research** will be listed under "Altick, Richard D." and under the title as well. If the library has a thorough card catalog this book will also be listed under a subject heading, such as "Literature: Research."

Many libraries have one catalog only, with all types of listings in it, alphabetized from A to Z. Others have three catalogs, one each for author, title, and subject. In addition, some libraries have separate sections of their catalogs reserved for periodicals, or serials, listings. (**Serial** means any publication that is put out in a **series**, such as most magazines, some series of books that are published a volume at a time, or books such as the yearly **Who's Who**.) There are also cross-references that tell the user to **see** or **see under** another entry for related materials.

The card catalog will almost always give the researcher a starting point. It gives a brief description of the contents of each publication, as well as other basic information, such as edition, publisher's name, and date of publication. If the researcher finds a book he or she wants, he copies down the call number, which is really a series of numbers in the upper left corner of the card which both identify the book and tell where it is in the library.

If the "open shelf" system is used, the shelves are open to all, and most of the books in the library are obtained by self-service. Either the librarian or a printed diagram will direct the researcher to the shelf or alcove where the book is kept, and from there he or she will follow alphabetically and numerically until he comes to it. If the "closed system" is used, the researcher fills out a call slip for the book, writing the call number on it, and presents this slip at the circulation desk. One of the library staff will then get the book for him.

THE REFERENCE ROOM

Although the card catalog is the starting point and the first major tool in the library, the reference room is its real heart and is a second major tool. It is there that most of the basic volumes of considerable importance are found. Books in the reference room may not be taken from the library, however, but must be used only in the reference section, the main reading room, or occasionally in other designated areas. This is because the reference room contains indispensable research volumes that are in constant demand and must always be on hand. Fundamental among these volumes are the indexes to articles in magazines, journals, and other sources. These indexes are an almost inexhaustible storehouse of information and also supply clues to lead the researcher forward.

There are, for example, such references as **Books in Print** which can tell one whether a desired book is not only on library shelves but is also still being printed and available to buy.

AND A FINAL NOTE ABOUT THIS BOOK

Two other points should be noted about the arrangement of this book. One is that the index should be freely consulted. If a specific author, work, or period is in question, the index will be the quickest way to find all references to it, especially in a work of this sort where at times one title might fit under two or three entries in the Contents. Cross-references are therefore, for the most part, indicated in the index.

The other point, and a most important one, is that entries in different chapters are presented in one of three ways. In some chapters, for example, all entries are alphabetical. In others, they are chronological. In still others, the importance of some works makes an arrangement other than the foregoing the most logical.

The book itself is arranged so that it moves from the general to the specific—as can be seen by the Contents. It covers all types of source materials on all types and periods of literature, and finishes with chapters on concordances (definitions are given in the chapters), professional organizations, and the increasingly popular nonprint media. A list of commonly used abbreviations of sources most frequently consulted, as well as a number of other abbreviations related to the field, is included immediately following the Contents and preceding this Note. The Afterword may be of special interest to many readers, and may even hold a surprise or two.

1. Standard Basic Sources

Probably all works published, including those still in the process of being printed, are listed in some index in the library. And there are all kinds of indexes on all kinds of subjects. Although there are many index sources limited to the field of English literature, there are also many limited to other fields, as well as many that cover all subject areas including English literature. Knowledgeable English students at all levels should be familiar with the following guides, which cover all areas in their field from books through nonprint media—as shown in the Contents. Entries are listed by grouping.

GUIDES TO BOOK PUBLICATIONS

Books in Print. New York: Bowker, 1948-

This work, now divided into two separate volumes—one alphabetized by author, the other by title—gives all the essential data for books which are still in print. (That is, those books that are still being printed and that are available for purchase.) Price and publisher's name and address are given so that the book may be ordered or checked in another library. In the majority of cases the year of publication is also provided. **Books in Print** includes textbooks and many paperbacks and usually indicates editors and translators.

Subject Guide to Books in Print. New York: Bowker, 1957-

This companion to **Books in Print** lists fundamental information (author, title, publisher, place of publication, etc.) under subject headings; for instance, all books currently in print about A. E. Housman are listed under the heading of A. E. Housman. The **Subject Guide** furnishes a quick and reliable guide to available books on a particular topic.

Paperbound Books in Print. New York: Bowker, 1958-

This compilation is now published three times a year and classifies paperbacks into three well-organized indexes—title, author, and subject. It supplements **Books in Print** by being much more comprehensive in its listing of paperback titles and by including materials for the mass market along with the more quality publications.

Cumulative Book Index. New York: H. W. Wilson, 1898-

This work lists as many books published in the English language as it can possibly locate and attempts to keep a yearly recording of the essential facts of publication, especially author, title, place and date of publication, and publisher. The volumes serve as supplements to the **United States Catalog** (see following entry).

United States Catalog. New York: H. W. Wilson, 1899-

These volumes record books published with listings under author, title, and subject. This standard reference goes further than the **Cumulative Book Index** in that it attempts to record privately printed books, most state and national government publications, and other items not listed elsewhere. Used in association with the **Cumulative Book Index** it records the necessary publishing data about most books issued since 1898.

MARC (MAchine Readable Catalog) tapes.

MARC tapes are weekly listings on computer tape of books newly cataloged by the Library of Congress. Although the MARC computer file information is available in relatively few libraries, it is mentioned here because of its importance as a source of current information on new book publications.

Because of the time required to receive, process, and organize information, most printed guides (including the majority of those mentioned in this chapter) are of necessity published months or even years after the publication of the original work that they index. Therefore, if one is seeking current information about newly published books—worldwide—the MARC tapes are an indispensable resource.

GUIDE TO ARTICLES IN MAGAZINES AND JOURNALS

Readers' Guide to Periodical Literature. New York: H. W. Wilson, 1900-

This is the best-known magazine index, inasmuch as it refers to the most popular periodicals, such as **Harper's, New Yorker, Saturday Review, The Atlantic, Time**, etc. The **Readers' Guide** is arranged alphabetically by author and subject, with reference to the name of the journal and the particular volume, date, and pages. For example, if a reader wishes to gather material written by H. M. Tomlinson, he or she looks up Tomlinson's name in each of the collected volumes of the index as well as in the recent bimonthly and annual compilations. The references are presented concisely; for instance, in volume 20 one finds the following entry under Tomlinson's name:

Ship herself, Holiday, 20:54-5 July '56.

This means that the Tomlinson piece was in the July 1956 issue of **Holiday** magazine, in volume 20, on pages 54 and 55. Some periodical titles are abbreviated, but the abbreviations are explained in the front of the index.

Readers' Guide is published twice a month, except during July and August, and has frequent cumulations, with annual and two-year compilations being the easiest to consult. Except for very contemporary material and a few exceptional topics, the popular magazines which **Readers' Guide** indexes are not helpful for literary study. Students would waste time looking for important material about Shakespeare, the Gothic novel, etc., in such sources.

For material of a similar nature appearing before 1900, the following two books function, in effect, as predecessors to the **Readers' Guide**.

Nineteenth Century Readers' Guide to Periodical Literature, New York: H. W. Wilson, 1890-1899.

This work covers magazine material in the last ten years of the nineteenth century. It includes author entries and cross-references not found in **Poole's Index** (see next entry). It is both an author and subject index to the most popular magazines published during the period covered and indexes several periodicals not included in Poole, e.g., **Harper's, Yellow Book**, and **PMLA**.

Poole's Index to Periodical Literature, 1802-1907. 6 vols. Reprint, Gloucester, Mass.: Peter Smith Publisher, 1963.

This is the standard index for nineteenth-century journals and magazines. The original **Poole's Index** covered material to 1881. Five supplements appeared which indexed material up to January 1, 1907. Although **Poole's Index** is particularly helpful for gathering data concerning the period covered, it is a subject index only; no author entries are given. The dates of a particular article must be determined from a special table at the beginning of the index, and several of the entries are very sketchy. Many of the magazines indexed by Poole are difficult to obtain. **Poole's Index** must suffice for 1802-1890, but for the period thereafter the reader is better advised to use the two earlier forms of the **Readers' Guide** (see the two preceding entries). A badly needed author index to Poole is now available: C. Edward Wall, ed., **Cumulative Author Index for Poole's Index to Periodical Literature, 1802-1906** (Ann Arbor, Mich.: Pierian Press, 1971).

Annual Bibliography of English Language and Literature. Cambridge, Engl.: Cambridge University Press, 1921-

Often referred to as the **MHRA Bibliography** since it is issued under the auspices of the Modern Humanities Research Association (described in Chapter 23), this is an extremely valuable bibliographic tool that surveys literature from the Old English period up to and including the twentieth century. Although it lists mainly magazines and journals, it does list some books, too. It also mentions the latest work in such areas as language and speech, dictionaries and grammars, literary history and criticism, etc., and bibliographic material from many areas of the world. There is a section on American literature. Originally issued by Cambridge University Press, the volumes are now printed by the MHRA.

Index to Little Magazines. Denver: Alan Swallow, 1943-

"Little" magazines are small-circulation, intellectually oriented magazines that are usually sponsored by a college, university, or specialized group. This index is an author and subject index to a selected list of these little magazines, such as **Fugitive, Four Quarters, Accent, Epoch, Prairie Schooner, Southwest Review, Beloit Poetry Journal, Colorado Quarterly**, and the **Transatlantic Review**. Most of these periodicals publish interesting creative and critical works, and many famous authors have made their first appearance in print in such journals. Much important literary commentary about and sometimes by significant writers also appears in the little magazines. **Index to Little Magazines 1943-1947**, edited by Stephen Goode, was published by Alan Swallow's press in Denver in 1965. From 1948 to the present it has been continued by the Swallow Press (now in Chicago), with occasional compilations—about every two or three years. The latest issue, for 1966-1967, was published in 1970.

Stephen Goode has also carried the indexes back to 1900 by editing three important publications: **Index to American Little Magazines 1920-1939** (Troy, N.Y.: Whitston Publishing Co., 1969), **Index to Little Magazines 1940-1942** (New York: Johnson Reprint Co., 1967), and **Index to American Little Magazines 1900-1919** (3 vols., Troy, N.Y.: Whitston Publishing Co., 1974).

These three volumes include additions and corrections to previous indexes compiled by Goode and also index several British and Continental magazines for the years 1900-1950; thus, the usefulness of this compilation is enhanced considerably.

(Modern Language Association) **MLA International Bibliography**, or **PMLA** (Publications of the Modern Language Association) **Annual Bibliography**, 1921-

Starting with 1922, **PMLA** began publishing an annual bibliography of English and American literature which has grown to a status of truly deserved prestige and value. Before 1956 only American scholarship was included, but the bibliography was subsequently expanded to cover many foreign literatures. It appears as a separate unit of the **PMLA** journal and has now (as of 1962) acquired the appropriate title of **MLA International Bibliography**, although it is still frequently referred to as **PMLA**. The **Bibliography** lists mainly magazine and journal articles, but it does include some books, too. The yearly volumes have been bound separately and reprints have been issued so that now most libraries have the **MLA** bibliography issues easily available for consultation. Literature is indexed according to country of linguistic origin, e.g., American, English, Medieval Latin, and under periods, e.g., Eighteenth Century, Twentieth Century.

The **MLA International Bibliography** publishes four different indexes. Volume 1 treats of general literature (aesthetics, literary criticism and theory, etc.) as well as English, American, Medieval, Neo-Latin, and Celtic literature. Volume 2 contains sections on European, Asian, African, and Latin-American literature. Volume 3 is devoted to linguistics, and volume 4 contains listings on pedagogy in modern foreign languages. These bibliographies can be obtained separately and are also available together in a library edition.

A special reminder for using the **MLA** is in order. The reader should be sure to get the full title of the abbreviated journal name from the list at the beginning of the volume because many of these abbreviations are used only by **MLA**. See also the following entry.

MLA (Modern Language Association) **Abstracts**, 1970-

This is an annual volume covering the various national literatures, including such areas as linguistics, that are listed in the **MLA International Bibliography**. The contents of a selected group of articles in scholarly journals are summarized so that the reader can determine whether he or she wants to peruse the complete article. A general picture of current scholarship about an author or topic can also be gleaned from these abstracts.

From time to time the question for which one needs an answer is even more basic: Does a journal exist that covers a particular author, or period? For example, is there a periodical on Dickens? (There is.) The following indexes can sometimes be especially helpful in answering such questions.

Social Sciences and Humanities Index. New York: H. W. Wilson, 1965-

This is an indispensable author and subject index to periodicals in the humanities. Such journals as **American Speech, Hudson Review, Modern Language Review, PMLA, Sewanee Review, Speculum**, are indexed. As this sampling indicates, the **Social Sciences and Humanities Index** deals with significant intellectual periodicals and is international in scope. Especially valuable is the coverage of important British journals. Presently published four times a year, with annual bound cumulations, this compilation is a continuation of the **International Index** which began surveying publications in 1907. The title was changed to the current one with volume 19 (April 1965-March 1966 issue). This and the **Readers' Guide** are the two most frequently used magazine indexes.

Ulrich's International Periodical Directory. New York: Bowker, 1932-

Originally called **Ulrich's Periodical Directory**, this reference work lists alphabetically, under general subject headings (e.g., literature), almost every journal and magazine published in the United States and England, although other countries are also represented. Over 50,000 periodicals are currently recorded. It gives the title of the periodical, the price, the publisher, and notes the frequency and place of publication. It also lists new periodicals and records the termination of others.

For works more sharply focused on periodicals geared to English students and scholars, and more convenient for regular use, see the two following listings.

Meserole, Harrison T., and Carolyn James Bishop, comp. **Directory of Journals & Series in the Humanities: A Data List of the Periodical Sources on the Master List of the MLA International Bibliography.** New York: Modern Language Association, 1970.

This monograph gives basic information about the majority of journals indexed by MLA and gives the abbreviations used for periodical titles.

Gerstenberger, Donna, and George Hendrick, eds. **Third Directory of Periodicals Publishing Articles on English and American Literature.** Chicago: Swallow Press, 1970.

As the title indicates, this book is especially useful for those who wish to find a suitable journal in which to publish their own research.

GUIDES TO NEWSPAPERS

The New York Times Index, 1851-

This famous compilation serves as a subject index to material which has appeared in **The New York Times**. Now published twice a month with annual cumulations, this index is especially helpful in determining dates and for locating book reviews, drama reviews, and news and obituary material about famous authors. Eventually the index will be extended back to include all issues of the **Times** from its initial appearance to the present.

The **Times** of London also publishes an index to its materials, arranged by subject, and covering the years from 1906 to the present.

Several other newspaper indexes also cover national, international, and local papers.

OTHER GUIDES TO LITERATURE

Bibliographic Index. New York: H. W. Wilson, 1937-

This is an index of bibliographies that appear in periodicals, pamphlets, and a selected list of books. First published in 1945, the initial cumulation covered the 1937-1942 period and has been published regularly since that time. It is presently published in April and August and in a bound cumulation each December. The index covers bibliographies in all areas of study and lists author as well as subject bibliographies. Even though this is a cumulative bibliography of bibliographies, it omits many bibliographies published in various journals, pamphlets, and books and is consequently anything but complete.

Essay and General Literature Index. New York: H. W. Wilson, 1900-

This standard reference work is an author and subject index to individual essays and articles in books—anthologies and similar collections. First published in 1934, covering 1900-1933, this reference source originally indexed several years in one volume. Thus, volume 2 indexed 1934-1940; volume 3, 1941-1947, and so on. Since 1959 the **Essay and General Literature Index** has appeared twice a year, with an annual cumulative volume. Author, subject, and title entries are arranged alphabetically. If a reader is interested in Dylan Thomas, for example, he can find several entries under Thomas's name in the 1971 compilation (to choose one volume at random). One such reference is:

Amis, K. An evening with Dylan Thomas
In Amis, K. What became of Jane Austen? And other
questions p 57-62

At the end of the **Essay and General Literature Index** there is a list of the anthologies and collections indexed, giving the name of the publisher, the date of publication, and other necessary data. In the example used, Harcourt, Brace published Kingsley Amis's collection **What Became of Jane Austen? And other Questions**.

The **Essay and General Literature Index** is a useful guide, but it occasionally overlooks some worthwhile material. A new author, editor, and title index to all seven permanent cumulations is now available—**Essay and General Literature Index: Works Indexed 1900-1969** (New York: H. W. Wilson, 1973).

BASIC CATALOGS

A Catalog of Books Represented by Library of Congress Printed Cards Issued to July 31, 1942. 167 vols. Ann Arbor: Edwards, 1942-1946.

This massive reference tool reprints facsimiles of the cards in the catalog of the Library of Congress, with all the important bibliographic information these cards provide, including their

Library of Congress call numbers. The book's location in other libraries is also indicated. A 42-volume supplement of cards from 1942 to the end of 1947 was issued in 1948.

Edwards continued the project by publishing **The Library of Congress Author Catalog** (1948-1952) and **The National Union Catalog: Author List** (1953-). The project is continually being updated. There are also separate volumes, published by Edwards, registering additional locations where books may be found.

The National Union Catalog: Pre-1956 Imprints. London: Mansell, 1968-

This multivolumed cumulative author listing also presents facsimiles of Library of Congress printed cards. Over 600 volumes are planned, but at present only the letter M has been reached. These volumes will supersede the previous catalog volumes, but must, of course, be supplemented by post-1956 publications.

Union List of Serials in Libraries of the United States and Canada. New York: H. W. Wilson, 1927.

There have been numerous supplements to this 1927 reference work, and since 1950 it has continued with the designation **New Serial Titles**, originally cosponsored by the Library of Congress and Bowker publishers. The most recent updating cumulates materials from 1950 to 1970 and has been published in four volumes (New York: Bowker, 1973).

These many volumes (from 1927 to 1973) give the location, volume number, and date of the periodicals and journals so that, if need be, a researcher can contact the library that holds the issues he or she requires and obtain them on microfilm if he cannot visit the library in person. This work is extremely useful for finding difficult-to-locate issues of particular journals.

2. General Survey Materials

Inasmuch as both English and American literature cover extensive stretches of time and include thousands of authors and writings, and many survey courses move roughly from **Beowulf** to Dylan Thomas and from Ben Franklin to Wallace Stevens, it is helpful for the researcher to have a list of some essential survey materials. These materials are more specific than those in the preceding chapter and more general than those in the chapters to come. The sources listed below were selected not only to be useful in themselves but to lead readers to further sources.

ENGLISH LITERATURE—OVERALL BIBLIOGRAPHY

Bateson, F. W. **A Guide to English Literature.** 2d ed. Garden City, N.Y.: Doubleday Anchor, 1968.

This is an extremely handy survey of critical and bibliographical materials dealing with British literature from the earliest period to the twentieth century. Bateson gives reading lists for each era, comments on most of his entries, and provides brief but stimulating introductions to all the major literary periods except the present century. Bateson's volume is especially recommended as a starting point for all literature students.

Bateson, F. W., ed. **The Cambridge Bibliography of English Literature**. 4 vols. Cambridge, Engl.: Cambridge University Press, 1941.

The **CBEL** has traditionally been the starting point for gathering bibliography on British literature from 600 to 1900. It presents many basic and important references, but it also omits some worthwhile material. It is especially valuable in furnishing data on genres, movements, and the lesser authors, since this information might well be overlooked elsewhere. It gives titles and publication dates and notes selected secondary studies. It is definitely a work to be consulted, but with the realization that much secondary material is omitted and that the new edition (**NCBEL**) takes precedence (see second citation following). Volume 4 consists solely of an index to the three previous volumes.

A supplement (volume 5), edited by George Watson, was
published by Cambridge University Press in 1957 and is devoted
to listing material which has been published since the original
CBEL appeared. It is a useful tool, but again omits many important
references.

Watson, George, ed. **The Concise Cambridge Bibliography of English
Literature**. 2d ed. Cambridge, Engl.: Cambridge University Press,
1965.

This is a condensed version of the **CBEL** and adds material on the
first part of the twentieth century (to 1950). Highly selective in
choosing materials for inclusion, Watson at least accurately lists
the works published by each writer. The condensed **CBEL** is
extremely skimpy and incomplete on secondary materials.

Watson, George, ed. **The New Cambridge Bibliography of English
Literature**. 4 vols. Cambridge, Engl.: Cambridge University Press,
1969-1974.

This is a thorough revision of the **CBEL**. Volume 1 covers 600 to
1660; volume 2, 1660-1800; volume 3, 1800-1900; and volume 4,
1900-1950. George Watson edited the first three volumes, and I. R.
Willison edited volume 4. Although the print is tiny and the overall
format crowded and somewhat haphazard at times, the new **CBEL**
is a vital, indispensable reference work which can be strongly
recommended. It records significant biographical materials,
collections of works, bibliographies, collections of letters, critical
articles, and other salient aspects of literary study.

THE OLD ENGLISH PERIOD

Bonser, Wilfrid. **An Anglo-Saxon and Celtic Bibliography (450-
1087)**. 2 vols. Berkeley: University of California Press, 1957.

This bibliography of the cultural, social, and historical materials
of the Anglo-Saxon period covers scholarship completed up to the
end of 1953. While it must be supplemented for post-1953 research,
it gives an excellent checklist on geography, archaeology, and
ecclesiastical, political, and local history—indeed, on all phases of
Anglo-Saxon life.

Greenfield, Stanley B. **A Critical History of Old English Literature**.
New York: New York University Press, 1965.

Readers interested in a well-researched and -balanced survey of
the Anglo-Saxon period must examine this book. In addition to its
scholarly handling of material, it has the virtue of presenting the

most current work. Students dealing with the Anglo-Saxon and Middle English periods should also use Greenfield's annotated bibliography of the same periods, which is found in David M. Zesmer's **Guide to English Literature from Beowulf through Chaucer and Medieval Drama** (New York: Barnes & Noble, 1961).

Heusinkveld, Arthur, and Edwin Bashe. **A Bibliographical Guide to Old English: A Selective Bibliography of the Language, Literature, and History of the Anglo-Saxons**. Iowa City: University of Iowa Press, 1931.

> This study of individual Anglo-Saxon works, e.g., "Juliana," gives bibliography, text references, secondary articles, and translated versions. It also gives bibliographies on law, arts, crafts, manuscripts, collections, versification, etc. Although it is very useful, it must, of course, be supplemented by contemporary research material, such as Greenfield's study (see preceding entry), Zesmer's **Guide**, and checklists published in the **MLA International Bibliography**.

THE MIDDLE ENGLISH PERIOD

Billings, Anna H. **A Guide to the Middle English Metrical Romances**. New York: Henry Holt, 1901.

> Originating as a Yale Studies in English project, this volume deals with both English and Germanic legends. It also considers the cycles of Arthur and of Charlemagne. Only the most significant romances are examined. Billings takes each romance, e.g., Joseph of Arimathea, gives the story, discusses the origin, and explains what the critics say about it. Meter, dialect, and similar topics are treated, and a bibliography of criticism is presented. Even though this work must be supplemented by modern research, readers will find it convenient and informative.

Brown, Carleton. **A Register of Middle English Religious and Didactic Verse**. 2 vols. Oxford: Oxford University Press, 1916, 1920.

> This reference, which preceded the Brown and Robbins **Index** (see following entry), is organized on the same format. The location of the manuscript is indicated, critical comments are recorded, and a bibliography is given. The **Register** is another invaluable reference tool.

Brown, Carleton, and Rossell Hope Robbins. **The Index of Middle English Verse**. New York: Columbia, 1943.

> This volume concentrates on secular verse and includes some religious poems that were omitted from the **Register** (see preceding entry). It lists the first line, describes the poem, gives

the location of the poem, and then gives a bibliography of scholarly articles or comments. For example, the poem "A Mercy fortune have pitee on me," is described as "A complaint against Fortune—3 stanzas rime royal with 2 line refrain." The manuscript is next located at Cambridge University (with catalog designation), and then a brief bibliography is given; e.g., "Mac-Cracken has written about this verse in **PMLA**." This work is an extremely valuable and necessary guide in its field.

Addenda and corrections and some texts from before 1943 that had been overlooked may be found in Rossell Hope Robbins and John L. Cutler's **Supplement to the Index to Middle English Verse** (Lexington: University of Kentucky Press, 1965).

Farrar, Clarissa, and Austin Evans. **Bibliography of English Translations from Medieval Sources**. New York: Columbia, 1946.

Farrar and Evans list English translations (editions, publishers, dates) from medieval sources, indicate what sections of the original works are translated, and offer comments on the relationship of one translation to another. Brief annotations about the contents of individual works are also furnished.

Fisher, John H., ed. **The Medieval Literature of Western Europe: A Review of Research, Mainly 1930-1960**. New York: New York University Press, 1966.

This project was undertaken by the Modern Language Association and various specialists contributed chapters to it. In addition to presenting sections on English literature, the work deals with literature in French, German, Old Norse, and other languages. Most scholarly in approach, the essays focus on some main texts and criticism. They tend to be sketchy, however, and must be supplemented by other bibliographies.

Griffith, Dudley. **Bibliography of Chaucer 1908-1953**. Seattle: University of Washington Press, 1955.

This superb bibliography includes material from earlier Chaucer bibliographies (one by Griffith himself) and also supplements Spurgeon's work (see entry below) in its "Influence and Allusions" section. It is updated by William R. Crawford's **Bibliography of Chaucer 1954-1963** (Seattle: University of Washington Press, 1967). The most recent Chaucerian bibliography, however, is to be found in the annual checklist published in the **Chaucer Review** (Pennsylvania State University Press).

Rowland, Beryl, ed. **Companion to Chaucer Studies**. New York: Oxford University Press, 1968.

This handbook presents essays by different scholars on Chaucer's prosody, imagery, rhetoric, astrology, etc., and studies his individual works. An extensive and pertinent bibliography is given for each essay.

Severs, J. Burke, ed. **Recent Middle English Scholarship and Criticism: Survey and Desiderata**. Pittsburgh: Duquesne University Press, 1971.

This survey examines four literary topics: **Piers Plowman, Sir Gawain and the Green Knight**, Middle English romances, and Chaucer's **Canterbury Tales**. It presents the latest scholarly trends, evaluates recent research, and suggests directions for new studies. It is a most informative and useful survey and has extensive footnotes.

Spurgeon, Caroline. **500 Years of Chaucer Criticism and Allusion, 1357-1900**. 3 vols. Reprint, New York: Russell and Russell, 1960.

Spurgeon's work first appeared from 1908 to 1917 in the Chaucer Society Publications and was published by the Cambridge University Press in 1925. It is an amazing gathering of Chaucerian materials of all types. An outline of the fluctuations of Chaucer's literary reputation during the past 500 years is included. Spurgeon also examines allusions and criticisms of Chaucer and studies qualities ascribed to him, the evolution of his biography, etc. The volumes include French and German references. To some degree, Spurgeon's work has been overshadowed by the new discoveries and interpretations of modern scholarship, yet it will never cease to be an essential storehouse of Chaucerian potpourri.

Wells, John E. **A Manual of the Writings in Middle English, 1050-1400**. New Haven: Yale University Press, 1916.

This is the classic study and bibliography of Middle English literature. It endeavors to treat all writings of that era. It gives probable date and form of each manuscript, the dialect in which it was composed, and source or sources, bibliography and commentary, and, in some cases, abstracts. Over the years, starting in 1923, various supplements have been published. The supplements contain additions and corrections and any changes arising from the discovery of new information. The **Ninth Supplement**, with revisions, compiled by Beatrice Brown, Eleanor

Heningham, and Francis Utley, was published by Yale University
Press in 1952.
   A revised edition is now in progress, and four volumes of it have
appeared: J. Burke Severs and others, eds., **A Manual of the
Writings in Middle English, 1050-1500** (New Haven: Connecticut
Academy of Arts and Sciences, vol. 1, 1967; vol. 2, 1970; vol. 3,
1972; vol. 4, 1973). Albert E. Hartung is the general editor for
volumes 3 and 4. The new edition is both a rewriting and an
expansion of the original **Manual**, with bibliographies updated
and modern evaluations incorporated. These volumes also add the
fifteenth century as subject matter.

THE RENAISSANCE AND THE SEVENTEENTH
AND EIGHTEENTH CENTURIES

Three volumes are especially useful in studying sixteenth-,
seventeenth-, and eighteenth-century materials. These books are
in the Oxford History of English Literature series (see Chapter 8):
C. S. Lewis, **English Literature in the Sixteenth Century
(excluding Drama)**; Douglas Bush, **English Literature in the
Earlier Seventeenth Century, 1600-1660**; and Bonamy Dobree,
English Literature in the Early Eighteenth Century.

One should also consult the yearly Renaissance bibliography
published (until 1969) in **Studies in Philology**, the bibliography in
Studies in English Literature, 1500-1900, and the annual
checklist covering research for the 1660-1800 period published in
Philological Quarterly. Also of value is the material listed in
"Abstracts of Recent Studies" and published in each issue of
Seventeenth-Century News since 1943. Some other basic works
in this area include the following.

Bond, Donald F. **The Age of Dryden.** New York: Appleton-Century-
Crofts, Meredith, 1970. Now issued by AHM Publishing Corporation,
Northbrook, Ill.

   This is a convenient, useful introductory bibliography about
   Dryden and the other writers of his era. In addition, some basic
   guideposts in historical, social, and cultural background are listed
   as well as material relating to literary criticism. As Professor
   Bond observes, this checklist must be supplemented by the **CBEL**,
   the **MHRA Annual Bibliography**, and other more-thorough

volumes. It is, however, one of the best books in the Goldentree
Bibliographies in Language and Literature series.

Dyson, A. E., ed. **The English Novel**. London: Oxford University
Press, 1974.

One of Oxford's Select Bibliographical Guides, this book presents
an excellent introduction to various novelists. Each chapter is
written by an acknowledged expert. The novelists studied are
Bunyan, Defoe, Swift, Richardson, Fielding, Sterne, Smollett,
Scott, Austen, Thackeray, Dickens, Trollope, the Brontës, George
Eliot, Hardy, Henry James, Conrad, Forster, Lawrence, and Joyce.

Dyson, A. E., ed. **English Poetry**. London: Oxford University Press,
1971.

This is one of the volumes in the Oxford Select Bibliographical
Guides series. Each chapter is devoted to a particular writer and is
compiled by a specialist in the subject matter. Recommended
readings are described under the following headings: texts,
critical studies and commentary, biographies, bibliographies, and
background reading. A final overall bibliography is then given at
the end of each chapter. The poets analyzed are Chaucer, Spenser,
Donne, Herbert, Milton, Marvell, Dryden, Pope, Blake,
Wordsworth, Coleridge, Byron, Shelley, Keats, Tennyson,
Browning, Arnold, Hopkins, Yeats, and Eliot. This is a valuable
and basic introduction to the work of these writers.

Hanford, James Holly, and James Taaffe. **A Milton Handbook**. 5th ed.
New York: Appleton-Century-Crofts, 1970.

Although there are excellent handbooks about many writers, this
guide to Milton is unrivaled. It includes just about every
significant fact about Milton's life and literary works and supplies
references for further study.

Huckabay, Calvin. **John Milton, A Bibliographical Supplement, 1929-
1957**. Pittsburgh: Duquesne University Press, 1960.

This listing of Milton research includes masters' theses and
doctoral dissertations as well as many book reviews. Many of the
entries are annotated. The volume supplements David Stevens's
Reference Guide to Milton from 1800 to the Present Day (Chicago:
The University of Chicago Press, 1930). Practically all the
bibliography items are annotated. Stevens's book overlaps with
Harris Fletcher's **Contributions to a Milton Bibliography 1880-
1930** (Urbana: University of Illinois Press, 1931), which adds
some bibliographical material that Stevens doesn't have.

McNeir, Waldo, and Foster Provost. **Annotated Bibliography of Edmund Spenser, 1937-1960**. Pittsburgh: Duquesne University Press, 1962. [The 1975 revision takes the bibliography to 1972.]

This is a very important study for Spenser scholarship that has added value because of its annotations. It continues the work of Dorothy Atkinson's **Edmund Spenser, A Bibliographical Supplement** (Baltimore: Johns Hopkins, 1937). Atkinson covered scholarship from 1923 to 1936 and gave a very thorough annotated checklist, following the lead of Frederic Carpenter's **A Reference Guide to Edmund Spenser** (Chicago: The University of Chicago Press, 1923), which is most useful even though the annotations are brief. Readers especially interested in Spenser should consult the **Spenser Newsletter**, published triannually by the University of Western Ontario since 1970.

Tannenbaum, Samuel A., and Dorothy R. Tannenbaum, eds. **Elizabethan Bibliographies**. New York: The authors, 1937-1947.

This immense undertaking comprises forty-one volumes with six supplements. The Tannenbaums give concise bibliographies of works by and about such figures as Marlowe, Jonson, Beaumont and Fletcher, Chapman, Lyly, Middleton, Kyd, Webster, Ford, Sidney, Montaigne, Tourneur, Herbert, and Herrick. Further, there are many volumes devoted to bibliographies of specific literary works—although these are limited to Shakespeare, e.g., **Macbeth, King Lear, The Merchant of Venice**, the sonnets, **Othello**. While these volumes must be updated by the checklists in the **Shakespeare Quarterly** and other materials mentioned elsewhere in this book, they furnish convenient collections of earlier scholarship.*

Nether Press has already begun to publish **Elizabethan Bibliographies Supplements** to the Tannenbaum material (London, 1967-). This is announced as an ongoing series. So far, supplements have been published on such writers as Webster, Jonson, Sidney, Marlowe, and Chapman. The Nether Press also plans to include bibliographies of some Elizabethan authors not covered in the Tannenbaum collection.

Tobin, James E. **Eighteenth Century English Literature and Its Cultural Background: A Bibliography**. New York: Fordham, 1939.

This is a fundamental bibliographical survey of important

*Shakespeare material is listed primarily in Chapter 12.

eighteenth-century materials. It covers history, politics, philosophy, criticism, and almost every other aspect of the Augustan Age. It is geared to filling gaps in the **CBEL**. If one is studying literary criticism and concepts (historical, political, philosophical, etc.) published prior to 1939, this is a helpful and authoritative volume. Post-1939 scholarship will be found in such cumulations as **PQ**, **SEL**, and **NCBEL**.

THE NINETEENTH CENTURY— ROMANTIC AND VICTORIAN PERIODS

Two classic works dealing with the Romantic period are mentioned first, below, followed by three covering the Victorian period.

Houtchens, C. W., and L. H. Houtchens, eds. **The English Romantic Poets and Essayists: A Review of Research and Criticism**. Rev. ed. New York: New York University Press, 1966.

Prepared under the auspices of the Modern Language Association and first published in 1957, this standard study reviews the most important and the latest information and criticism on Blake, Hazlitt, Scott, Southey, Campbell, Lamb, Moore, Landor, Hunt, and DeQuincey. A chapter on Carlyle appears in the 1966 revision. Excellent bibliographies are furnished for each of the writers studied.

Raysor, Thomas, and others, eds. **The English Romantic Poets: A Review of Research**. Rev. ed. New York: Modern Language Association, 1956.

This volume covers five authors: Wordsworth, Coleridge, Byron, Shelley, and Keats. In a series of essays, it provides essential data about bibliographies, editions, biographies, and historical and literary criticism, etc., relating to each writer. This work is exceedingly valuable in giving the principal data necessary to undertake further studies of these writers.

A third edition of this invaluable work has recently been issued, edited by Frank Jordan, Jr., called **The English Romantic Poets: A Review of Research and Criticism** (New York: Modern Language Association, 1972). This study brings the Raysor book up to date. In addition it emphasizes the new types of criticism developed in the last few years.

DeLaura, David, ed. **Victorian Prose: A Guide to Research**. New York: Modern Language Association, 1973.

Concentrating on Arnold, Carlyle, Ruskin, Pater, Newman, and other significant prose writers of the Victorian period, this guide presents the main themes and characteristics of their work and records the findings of modern scholarship. This is an important companion volume to the two following bibliographical items.

Faverty, Frederic E., ed. **The Victorian Poets: A Guide to Research**. 2d ed. Cambridge, Mass.: Harvard, 1969.

The Faverty book has established itself as an essential work in its field, with reviews of bibliography, scholarship, and criticism on Tennyson, Browning, Arnold, Hopkins, the pre-Raphaelites, Kipling, Housman, etc. In addition to evaluating materials on the major figures, it also expertly views the writing of minor poets, including Wilde and Stevenson.

Stevenson, Lionel, ed. **Victorian Fiction: A Guide to Research**. Cambridge, Mass.: Harvard, 1964.

This is another immensely important reference work that presents recent scholarly and perceptive critical thinking about Dickens, George Eliot, Thackeray, the Brontës, Trollope, Meredith, and other significant nineteenth-century novelists, along with material about editions, biographies, studies of individual novels, and bibliographies.

THE TWENTIETH CENTURY

Millett, Fred B. **Contemporary British Literature: A Critical Survey and 232 Author Bibliographies**. 3d rev. and enl. ed. New York: Harcourt, Brace, 1935.

This most recent printing is based upon the second edition by J. M. Manly and Edith Rickert. The relatively brief critical survey is completely subordinate to the bibliographies of the authors' works and the significant bibliographies of articles and reviews about each author. Many secondary bibliography items are of exceptional value because they are not easily accessible in any other work. The book review listings give a completeness that increases one's respect for the usefulness of this volume. The book deals with poets, novelists, dramatists, and writers of other genres.

Temple, Ruth Z., and Martin Tucker, eds. **A Library of Literary Criticism: Modern British Literature**. 3 vols. New York: Ungar, 1966.

Working from a concept derived from Moulton (see next entry), the editors of these volumes give excerpts from books, critical articles, and reviews about important twentieth-century British writers. The excerpts are intended to indicate some of the author's themes and characteristics as well as to give a general view of his writings. Detailed comments are also made about specific books. If used judiciously, these volumes can be a handy starting point for much more involved and in-depth reading and research.

ENGLISH AND AMERICAN LITERATURE

Moulton, Charles W., ed. **The Library of Literary Criticism of English and American Authors Through the Beginning of the Twentieth Century**. 4 vols. Abr., rev. ed. with additions by Martin Tucker. New York: Ungar, 1966.

Moulton published eight volumes of this reference work from 1901 to 1905. He selected excerpts from comments on English and American writers made in books, journals, and reviews and printed them. Many of the comments were trivial, obvious, and of no value, but some made worthwhile observations about the writer and his work. Martin Tucker abridged and updated the original volumes, pruned away the greater number of less significant views, and retained or inserted more-meaningful literary criticism. He also omitted some of the lesser authors found in Moulton and added new figures who deserved attention. Excerpts now included are drawn from publications up to 1964. This work should not be used alone but rather as a source of general information to lead the reader to more scholarly and comprehensive material.

Murphy, R., ed. **Contemporary Poets of the English Language**. New York: St. Martin's, 1970.

This large, one-volume reference work provides biographical and bibliographical data about living poets writing in English. Personal comments by the poets themselves are often included, and there are critical analyses and evaluations of the works of the more significant subjects. The volume is an extremely informative and indispensable reference and a companion volume to Vinson's **Contemporary Dramatists** and **Contemporary Novelists** (see below).

Riley, Carolyn, ed. **Contemporary Literary Criticism**. Detroit: Gale Research Company, 1973-

This is an ongoing refe.ence study which gives excerpts from literary criticism of the last twenty-five years about contemporary creative writing. Critical passages from many sources are quoted so that readers can receive a diversity of views about present-day poets, novelists, and playwrights. For purposes of this series, contemporary writers are those now living or who have died since January 1, 1960. As of 1975, three volumes of this encyclopedia of criticism have been published.

Vinson, James, ed. **Contemporary Dramatists**. New York: St. Martin's, 1973.

This book, which follows the same format as the St. Martin's volumes on contemporary poets and novelists, is an indispensable reference work on living playwrights. While the bibliographies and critical analyses are well presented, this study is perhaps most valuable for the personal remarks made by many of the authors listed.

Vinson, James, ed. **Contemporary Novelists**. New York: St. Martin's, 1972.

Thorough biographical and bibliographical data are given about modern novelists and short story writers from all parts of the world. Numerous critical comments are presented by scholarly experts. Many writers give their own personal comments about their work. This is a prime reference volume.

AMERICAN LITERATURE

Blanck, Jacob. **Bibliography of American Literature**. New Haven: Yale University Press, 1955-

A monumental work of scholarly bibliography, this project consists of descriptive bibliographies of all first editions and other separate publications by significant American authors (listed alphabetically) who died before 1931. Volume 6, the most recently published (1973), covers writers from Longstreet to Parsons.

Bryer, Jackson P., ed. **Fifteen Modern American Authors: A Survey of Research and Criticism**. Durham, N.C.: Duke, 1969.

This volume continues in the tradition of Stovall (described below). It presents critical and bibliographical data about the following moderns: Anderson, Cather, Crane, Dreiser, Eliot, Faulkner, Fitzgerald, Frost, Hemingway, O'Neill, Pound, Robinson, Steinbeck, Stevens, and Wolfe. Readers will find it an indispensable study.

Professor Bryer has edited a revised edition of this volume that presents addenda about the fifteen writers and includes a new section on William Carlos Williams: **Sixteen Modern American Authors; A Survey of Research and Criticism** (Durham, N.C.: Duke, 1972).

Curley, Dorothy Nyren, Maurice Kramer, and Elaine Kramer, eds. **A Library of Literary Criticism: Modern American Literature**. 3 vols., 4th enl. ed. New York: Ungar, 1969.

These volumes are arranged in the same manner as the Temple and Tucker, Moulton and Tucker reference works mentioned earlier in this chapter. Such figures as Allen Ginsberg, Randall Jarrell, Robert Lowell, Saul Bellow, James Baldwin, Jack Kerouac, etc., are considered and excerpts (about them and their writings) from journals, books, and reviews are given. Comments are usually on the writer's total literary production, with many excerpts dealing with individual novels and poems. The work is convenient and often useful in giving information and a brief perspective about writers, but it must be filled in by more in-depth studies and bibliographies.

Rees, Robert A., and Earl N. Harbert, eds. **Fifteen American Authors Before 1900: Bibliographic Essays on Research and Criticism**. Madison: The University of Wisconsin Press, 1971.

This excellent volume is an offshoot of the work by Stovall (see next entry). The writers considered are Adams, Bryant, Cooper, Crane, Dickinson, Edwards, Franklin, Holmes, Howells, Irving, Longfellow, Lowell, Norris, Taylor, and Whittier. Each author is studied under five basic headings: bibliography, editions, manuscripts, biography, and criticism. The major facts are given in each category. In addition, C. Hugh Holman and Louis Rubin have presented invaluable chapters entitled "The Literature of the Old South" and "The Literature of the New South." The highest praise must be showered on this volume. It is a primary starting point.

Stovall, Floyd, ed. **Eight American Authors: A Review of Research and Criticism**. New York: Norton, 1963.

This volume was first published by the Modern Language

Association in 1956. The Norton reprint adds a "Bibliographical Supplement: A Selective Check List, 1955-1962," compiled by J. Chesley Mathews. The eight authors studied are Poe, Emerson, Hawthorne, Thoreau, Melville, Whitman, Twain, and James, each of whom is reviewed by a different specialist. Evaluations and commentaries are given about editions, biographies, criticism, and bibliographies; and other data on philosophy, themes, literary reputations, etc., are usually added. This is a volume that can be described only in superlatives. It is imperative that anyone studying the writers in question consult Stovall's **Review**.

Woodress, James. **American Fiction, 1900-1950**. Detroit: Gale Research Company, 1974.

This is the first volume published in Gale's Information Guide Sources series. It gives a general bibliography of important background materials and then devotes chapters to individual writers. Each writer is studied under five basic categories: Bibliography and Manuscripts, Works of Fiction, Editions and Reprints, Biography, and Criticism. Basic bibliographical information is listed under each heading. This is a very helpful book which furnishes starting points, although it is occasionally unduly sketchy.

3. Serial Bibliographies

To gather as complete information as possible, one should be familiar with not only the **MLA International Bibliography** and the **MHRA Bibliography** mentioned in Chapter 1 (consult the Index for page numbers), but also with several others of these specialized serial bibliographies in one's subject area. Such bibliographies—which are sometimes known only to the well-informed graduate student or scholar—are storehouses of detailed information, not only exceedingly helpful in their own right but unrivaled in leading to additional data.

ENGLISH AND AMERICAN LITERATURE

The Year's Work in English Studies, 1921-   [Annually]

Sponsored by the English Association [England], this volume gives a survey of scholarship and research for each year. It mentions a selective number of articles and books and usually indicates the main points found in these materials. Few critical judgments are given, but this work performs a valuable service in that it provides information about much current research and presents the main elements involved in the scholarship it comments upon. **YWES** treats its material by units, e.g., "Old English Literature," "Middle English," "Chaucer," the "Renaissance," and "Shakespeare." It contains a separate section on American literature. As a publication emanating from England, it naturally tends to be much more informative about English works than about American ones. It has a convenient author and subject index. This reference guide has traditionally been late in publication; for example, **YWES** for 1969 was issued in 1971.

AMERICAN LITERATURE

American Literature Abstracts: A Review of Current Scholarship in the Field of American Literature, 1967-   [Semiannually]

This volume is published each June and December from the English Department of San Jose State College (California). While necessarily selective, it gives substantial summaries of the periodical articles cited. The abstracts are usually prepared by the authors of the original articles, which tends to ensure accuracy. They are arranged under the standard American literary period headings and are grouped by authors. A consensus of reviews of various books is also provided which gives this publication further value. The journal has been temporarily suspended since the volume 5, June 1972, issue.

"Articles on American Literature Appearing in Current Periodicals," in **American Literature**, 1929-   [Quarterly]

> **American Literature** publishes a checklist with the above title in each of its issues. Some of the bibliographical entries are very briefly annotated. The bibliography from 1929 to 1950, together with articles listed in the "American Bibliography" section of the **PMLA Annual Bibliography**, have been collected in Lewis Leary, ed., **Articles on American Literature, 1900-1950** (Durham, N.C.: Duke, 1954). An additional volume continues this compilation under one cover: Lewis Leary and others, eds., **Articles on American Literature, 1951-1968** (Durham, N.C.: Duke, 1970). This volume again compiles the quarterly checklists that appeared in **American Literature** from January 1951 through January 1968 and also includes items from before 1951 which were omitted from the earlier (**1900-1950**) volume. Other bibliographical items from the **PMLA** bibliographies, the **American Quarterly** checklists, etc., have also been incorporated in this compilation. These two books save researchers the time-consuming job of thumbing through every issue of **AL**, although for post-January 1968 to the present, individual issues must be consulted.

"Articles in American Studies," in **American Quarterly**, 1954- [Annually]

> This highly selective bibliography of literary and interdisciplinary studies (art, history, law, etc.) has been published annually in **American Quarterly** since 1955 and covers work of the previous year. Although most of the bibliographies in **American Literature** and in the two Leary books (see preceding entry) cover material mentioned here, this bibliography goes further and covers the period from 1969 on. It should be also checked for articles which might have been overlooked in other bibliographies. The listing is briefly, but usefully, annotated. Hennig Cohen has edited a cumulation of the annual bibliographies from this journal (1954-1968). His book, **Articles in American Studies, 1954-1968**, is published in two volumes by the Pierian Press, Ann Arbor, Michigan, 1972.

Woodress, James, ed. **American Literary Scholarship: An Annual**. Durham, N.C.: Duke, 1965-   [Annually]

Beginning with material published in 1963, these volumes are a survey of scholarship for the year treated. They take several major writers, such as Emerson, Thoreau, Hawthorne, Melville, James, Hemingway, etc., and have noted researchers discuss the present state of scholarship concerning them, comment on new books and articles, and make judgments and evaluations. The volumes also deal with genres, such as fiction and poetry, from all periods of American literature. They are modeled after the British **Year's Work in English Studies** (see first entry, this chapter) and are very helpful in giving a view of the latest trends and research information. Since some authors have debatable theories and crotchets, many of their comments must be taken accordingly.

For research published since 1968, J. Albert Robbins served as editor until 1973, when James Woodress resumed the role.

ENGLISH LITERATURE

The Middle Ages

"Bibliography of American Periodical Literature," in **Speculum**, 1934-1972. [Quarterly]

Speculum, a learned journal of medieval studies, has for thirty-eight years published in each issue a valuable checklist of periodical articles dealing with research on the Middle Ages. This bibliography, which last appeared in the October 1972 issue, should be supplemented with data from the **MLA International Bibliography**.

Parry, John J., and Margaret Schlauch, eds. **A Bibliography of Critical Arthurian Literature for the Years 1922-1929**. New York: Modern Language Association, 1931. [Irregularly; then annually]

A second volume of this work, covering the period 1930-1935, was published in 1936. Then, from 1936 until 1963, the "Bibliography of Critical Arthurian Literature" was published annually in **Modern Language Quarterly**. This is an especially fine compilation of Arthurian materials and covers a wide range of scholarship. For more recent data consult the **Bibliographical Bulletin of the International Arthurian Society (BBSIA)**.

The Renaissance

"Literature of the Renaissance," in **Studies in Philology**, 1917-1969. [Annually]

This excellent checklist was published yearly until it had to be discontinued. It, like the checklists of other particular periods, needs to be supplemented by the **MLA International Bibliography**.

"Recent Studies in Elizabethan and Jacobean Drama," in **Studies in English Literature, 1500-1900,** 1961-   [Quarterly; bibliography annually]

This bibliography is published in each spring issue of **Studies in English Literature.**

"Recent Studies in the English Renaissance," in **Studies in English Literature, 1500-1900,** 1961-   [Quarterly; bibliography annually]

This bibliography is published in each winter issue of **Studies in English Literature,** a journal published by Rice University. It contains a somewhat sketchy survey of some of the latest research in this period.

"Shakespeare: An Annotated Bibliography," in **Shakespeare Quarterly,** 1949-   [Annually]

Published beginning in 1950 and yearly thereafter, this bibliography is especially worthwhile because it is well annotated.

"The Year's Contributions to Shakespearian Study," in **Shakespeare Survey,** 1948-   [Annually]

This bibliography, which is compiled in essay form, appears annually. Not as complete or as thorough as the **Shakespeare Quarterly** bibliography, it nevertheless presents an important English point of view and is especially interesting in comments about critical and textual studies.

The Restoration, Eighteenth Century, and Pre-Romantic Period

"English Literature, 1660-1800: A Current Bibliography," in **Philological Quarterly,** 1925-   [Annually]

This checklist appears yearly in **PQ.** The bibliography for 1925-1949 has been extracted and published by Louis A. Landa and others, eds., **English Literature, 1660-1800: A Bibliography of Modern Studies** (2 vols. Princeton, N.J.: Princeton, 1950,1952). A third volume, edited by Arthur Friedman and others, and covering 1950-1955, has been published (1962) in the same Princeton series, as has a fourth volume, edited by Charles B. Woods and others, covering 1956-1959 (also 1962). This fourth volume contains an index to volumes 3 and 4. The **PQ** bibliographies are particularly distinguished for thoroughness and scholarly handling.

"Recent Studies in Restoration and Eighteenth Century," in **Studies in English Literature, 1500-1900,** 1961-   [Quarterly; bibliography annually]

This bibliography is published in each summer issue of **Studies in English Literature.**

The Romantic Period

The two bibliographies listed below present an excellent perspective of the Romantic era as well as of the authors who established the Romantic creed.

"Current Bibliography," in **Keats-Shelley Journal,** 1952- [Annually]

This bibliography, published yearly in **KSJ,** begins with data from the year 1950.

"The Romantic Movement: A Selective and Critical Bibliography," in **English Language Notes,** 1936-   [Annually]

This checklist began in **ELH** in 1937 and continued until 1949. In 1950 it was transferred to **Philological Quarterly** and continued there until 1964. Since 1967, it has been published annually as a supplement to the September issue of **English Language Notes,** which updates from 1964.

The Victorians

The first entry below is especially impressive and helpful.

"Victorian Bibliography," in **Victorian Studies,** 1933-   [Annually]

Beginning with data from the year 1932, this bibliography was published in **Modern Philology** from 1933 to 1957, and then shifted to **Victorian Studies,** where it has appeared regularly since 1958.

The material published from 1932 to 1964 has been collected in three volumes and published by The University of Illinois Press in Urbana: William D. Templeman, ed., **Bibliographies of Studies in Victorian Literature for the Thirteen Years 1932-1944** (1945); Austin Wright, ed., **Bibliographies of Studies in Victorian Literature for the Ten Years 1945-1954** (1956); and Robert Stack, ed., **Bibliographies of Studies in Victorian Literature for the Ten Years 1955-1964** (1967). Many of the items in these bibliographies are briefly described or annotated. The comprehensiveness of the "Victorian Bibliography" has always been impressive.

"Recent Studies in the Nineteenth Century," in **Studies in English Literature, 1500-1900**, 1961-   [Quarterly; bibliography annually]

This bibliographic essay dealing with both the Romantic and Victorian periods appears in each autumn issue of **Studies in English Literature**

The Twentieth Century

"Current Bibliography," in **Twentieth Century Literature**, 1955-[Quarterly]

Starting with the April 1955 issue, this journal has included a selected list of articles on contemporary authors and has annotated these materials. Because only a relatively small number of articles can be presented in each bibliography, the lists must be supplemented by the **MLA International Bibliography** and the lists in **Abstracts of English Studies**, etc.

English Literature in Transition, 1800-1920, 1957-   [Annually]

ELT publishes checklists, annotated bibliographies, and/or bibliographical data about writers such as H. G. Wells, Conrad, Galsworthy, and others who wrote during the late nineteenth and early twentieth centuries. For study of, or research on, writers of this period, this periodical is essential and required reading.

ANGLO-GERMAN LITERATURE

"Anglo-German Literary Bibliography," in **Journal of English and Germanic Philology**, 1935-   [Annually]

Although this journal was founded in 1897, it was not until the years 1935-1941 that the "Anglo-German Bibliography" was published. It was renewed in the 1946 volume and continues to the present under its current title. This is a definitive, mandatory checklist for students dealing with comparative literature. It is a splendid, comprehensive work.

4. Explication Checklists

Explication checklists are bibliographies of books, essays, and brief notes that interpret or explain the meaning of various words, passages, symbols, and themes found in such creative works as poems, plays, short stories, and novels. These books are extremely convenient for gathering a bibliography so that one can quickly locate and examine interpretations and analyses of specific literary works.

Checklists of explication are all arranged on one basic format. For example, in the Arms and Kuntz poetry explication volumes one can look up a specific poem (or poet) and find there a list of articles and books that help in analyzing it. There are over fifteen Keats poems, over thirty T. S. Eliot poems, several Emerson poems, etc., that have their own individual bibliographies. A writer's principal works are given followed by references to them. Under the heading of Donne's "The Ecstasy," for instance, one finds a list of articles in such journals as the **Sewanee Review** and **Philological Quarterly** as well as references to pertinent pages in William Empson's landmark work, **English Poetry**.

These explication checklist volumes are immensely helpful, but they must be used in conjunction with the **MLA International Bibliography** and other standard bibliographies so that additional and more recent material may be located. Since materials in some of the genre checklists overlap, more than one volume should be consulted.

DRAMA

Adelman, Irving, and Rita Dworkin, eds. **A Checklist of Critical Literature on Twentieth Century Plays**. Metuchen, N.J.: Scarecrow Press, 1967.

This bibliography, listing significant twentieth-century plays of all countries, gives general criticism as well as criticism of individual plays. For example, there are almost one hundred general items listed under Tennessee Williams, followed by bibliographical data listed under **Cat on a Hot Tin Roof, The Glass Menagerie, The Night of the Iguana, Period of Adjustment, The Rose Tattoo, A Streetcar Named Desire, Summer and Smoke**, and seven additional plays.

For contemporary playwrights, the Adelman and Dworkin volume is a standard reference tool. But it must be supplemented by Breed and Sniderman, Coleman and Tyler, and Palmer and Dyston (see the next entries), which contain many additional items.

Breed, Paul F., and Florence M. Sniderman, eds. **Dramatic Criticism Index, a Bibliography of Commentaries on Playwrights from Ibsen to the Avant Garde**. Detroit: Gale Research Company, 1972.

This work gives a selective index to criticism and analyses of twentieth-century playwrights and their plays. Bibliography and excerpts are given for each writer, and there is further material about the plays themselves. This is an extremely useful volume and the number of books and periodicals sources consulted is most impressive.

Coleman, Arthur, and Gary R. Tyler, eds. **Drama Criticism: A Checklist of Interpretation since 1940 of English and American Plays**. Denver: Alan Swallow, 1966.

This is a helpful guide to important bibliography for famous English and American plays. It covers not only early periods of English drama, e.g., Shakespeare and the Elizabethans, but also the most recent British and American plays. The book is arranged alphabetically by author.

A second volume by the same editors (**Drama Criticism: A Checklist of Interpretation since 1940 of Classical and Continental Plays**) was published by the Swallow Press (Chicago) in 1971. It is a bibliography of drama criticism published since 1940 about classical and Continental plays. Among the writers listed are

Euripides, Sophocles, Schiller, Sartre, Ibsen, Lorca, Goethe, Camus, Brecht, and Beckett. Like the first Coleman and Tyler volume, this project is well conceived and accomplished. The special value of these two checklists is that they include only very recent analyses.

Palmer, Helen H., and Anne Jane Dyson, eds. **American Drama Criticism: Interpretations, 1890-1965 Inclusive, of American Drama Since the First Play Produced in America**. Hamden, Conn.: Shoe String, 1967.

This work is to be used in conjunction with the other drama checklists. It contains both book and periodical material and is arranged alphabetically by playwrights. It includes much early material not found in the other checklists.

Palmer and Dyson have produced a companion volume, **European Drama Criticism** (Hamden, Conn.: Shoe String, 1968), which lists English and some foreign language criticism for the years 1900 to 1966 and is carried forward by a first supplement published in 1970. It is to be used as a complementary book to the second volume of **Drama Criticism** by Coleman and Tyler, as well as with Adelman and Dworkin, and Breed and Sniderman. Palmer and Dyson have also issued **European Drama Criticism: Supplement II** (Hamden, Conn.: Shoe String, 1974). This volume furnishes a bibliography for 1970, 1971, and 1972 and supplements the other volumes by the same authors.

Salem, James M. **A Guide to Critical Reviews**. New York: Scarecrow Press, 1966.

This volume indexes reviews of plays and theater productions by fifty-two American playwrights from O'Neill to Albee. It lists drama reviews from **The New York Times** and many popular periodicals. It enables a reader to find the original reviews, see how a play was received, and study different opinions and viewpoints. Salem has issued two additional volumes: **A Guide to Critical Reviews: Part II, The Musical from Rodgers-and-Hart to Lerner-and-Loewe** (1967), and **A Guide to Critical Reviews: Part III, British and Continental Drama from Ibsen to Pinter** (1968). These three books are without parallel for thoroughness in the field of the drama review.

FICTION

Bell, Inglis, and Donald Baird, eds. **The English Novel 1578-1956: A Checklist of Twentieth Century Criticisms**. Denver: Alan Swallow,

1958. Reprint, Hamden, Conn.: Shoe String, 1974.

Bell and Baird present bibliographies about individual novels from John Lyly's **Euphues** up to the work of recent figures such as Graham Greene. Although theirs is a highly selective bibliography, it is helpful as a starting point for research and general reading. From two to ten or so entries are listed under each novel. In addition to the bibliographies of individual novels, there is a general introduction to the study of the twentieth-century novel.

Gerstenberger, Donna, and George Hendrick, eds. **The American Novel 1789-1959: A Checklist of Twentieth Century Criticism.** Denver: Alan Swallow, 1961.

This is a highly useful reference tool, arranged alphabetically by author with bibliographic listings under the novels. It contains references both to periodical articles and to books about the works.

The same scholars have published a second checklist, containing additional items: **The American Novel: A Checklist of Twentieth Century Criticism on Novels Written Since 1789; Volume II, Criticism Written 1960-1968** (Chicago: Swallow Press, 1970). Both volumes are essential works of reference for gathering bibliography and commentary on the American novel.

Kearney, E. I., and L. S. Fitzgerald, eds. **The Continental Novel: A Checklist of Criticism in English, 1900-1966.** Metuchen, N.J.: Scarecrow Press, 1968.

This volume is similar to the two previous entries. It lists bibliography about important European works of fiction. The checklist is selective but useful, particularly since foreign-literature bibliographical material is not as easily accessible as is that for English language studies. The work includes English language criticism of novels in French, Russian, German, Italian, etc.

Palmer, Helen H., and Anne Jane Dyson. **English Novel Explication: Criticisms to 1972.** Hamden, Conn.: Shoe String, 1973.

A supplement to the original Bell and Baird volume mentioned earlier in this section, this reference guide lists criticism from 1958 to 1972 as well as some earlier items not mentioned by Bell and Baird. Although useful at times, the material is often unnecessarily skimpy and nonselective. It deals with British novels only.

Thurston, Jarvis, O. B. Emerson, Carl Hartman, and Elizabeth Wright, eds. **Short Fiction Criticism: A Checklist of Interpretation Since 1925 of Stories and Novelettes (American, British, Continental) 1800-1958**. Denver: Alan Swallow, 1960.

This volume lists articles and books containing explication of generally well-known short stories. It should be used in conjunction with the Walker volumes (see following entry) since they are much more comprehensive and up to date.

Walker, Warren S. **Twentieth Century Short Story Explication: Interpretations, 1900-1960, of Short Fiction Since 1800**. Hamden, Conn.: Shoe String, 1961.

This book is a bibliography of critiques and commentaries about short stories and covers criticism up to 1960. Walker has issued two supplementary volumes (both of which have been published by Shoe String); **Supplement 1** (1963) carries the bibliography of items up to April 1, 1963, and **Supplement 2** (1965) carries it through December 31, 1964. He has also published a revised second edition to his principal work: **Twentieth Century Short Story Explication: Interpretations, 1900-1966, of Short Fiction since 1800** (Hamden, Conn.: Shoe String, 1967).

All these volumes deal with short stories written by important European, English, and American authors. They list the authors— e.g., Willa Cather—and then list their individual stories—e.g., "Enchanted Bluff," "The Old Beauty," "Paul's Case," etc. Under the title of each short story, there are lists of articles and books which analyze and discuss that particular story.

POETRY

Arms, George, and Joseph Kuntz. **Poetry Explication: A Checklist of Interpretation Since 1925 of British and American Poems Past and Present**. New York: Morrow; Chicago: Swallow Press, 1950.

This is a listing of bibliographical items that analyze significant poems by British and American writers. Although, like all such checklists, it needs to be supplemented by serial bibliographies, **Poetry Explication** is a worthwhile reference.

Under the same title, Joseph Kuntz has edited a revised edition of this volume (Chicago: Swallow Press, 1962). It is an extension of the first edition and incorporates new bibliography (covering 1950-1959).

Cline, Gloria Stark, and Jeffrey A. Baker. **An Index to Criticisms of British and American Poetry**. Metuchen, N.J.: Scarecrow Press, 1973.

This work lists bibliography of criticisms of notable poems from the earliest English writing to the present. Although on occasion it does not cite as much criticism of a particular poem as desirable, all the references cited are in collections of criticism and/or in periodicals readily available in most college libraries.

Walcutt, Charles C., and J. Edwin Whitesell, eds. **The Explicator Cyclopedia**. 3 vols. Chicago: Quadrangle, 1966-1971.

This work, in three volumes, covers modern poetry; traditional poetry, medieval to late Victorian; and prose. It is a compilation of carefully selected brief essays and notes that are taken from the **Explicator** (see Chapter 19) and that explain various meanings, symbols, etc., of poetry and other genres. The explications are arranged alphabetically by author and by critic and are scholarly, succinct, and informative.

EPICS AND METRICAL ROMANCES

Coleman, Arthur. **Epic and Romance Criticism**. 2 vols. Searingtown, N.Y.: Watermill Publishers, 1973, 1974.

Volume 1 of this work is a checklist of bibliography (1940-1972) of English and American epics and metrical romances, while volume 2 (covering 1940-1973) deals with classical and Continental ones. Both books are highly recommended; they are scholarly and thoroughly researched. The sections on **The Canterbury Tales, Paradise Lost, The Faerie Queene**, and **The Aeneid** are particularly impressive.

5. Book Review Material

So many journals and newspapers have book columns or book sections that a comprehensive listing of them would be impossible. The six sources mentioned here are the ones most likely to be used frequently. In some respects, one of the sources—**Book Review Digest**—is in a class by itself; but the five others have also achieved prestige and are of considerable importance. Both the **Book Review Index** and **An Index to Book Reviews in the Humanities** include a vast number of sources that are found nowhere else.

PUBLICATIONS CONTAINING REVIEWS OR EXCERPTS FROM REVIEWS

Books Abroad. Norman: University of Oklahoma Press, 1927- [Quarterly]

> This publication is devoted to analysis of and comment on recent books published outside the continental United States. It also publishes articles on foreign writers of significance. Typical titles are "Two Novels from Kenya: James Ngugi," "Dürrenmatt's **The Visit** and Job," and "The Style of the New Spanish Novel." The work is incomparable for knowledge of and general news items about contemporary writers of other countries.

Book Review Digest. New York: H. W. Wilson, 1905-   [Monthly, except February, July]

> This reference work **BRD** also has yearly cumulations. A further cumulated index appears every five years. **BRD** indexes reviews of current fiction and nonfiction appearing in selected periodicals and journals, publishes excerpts from some book reviews, and also gives lists of additional reviews. It occasionally gives a brief prefatory description of the book's contents. A list of periodicals from which excerpts are taken or in which references are made is printed at the front of it. Each volume has a subject and title index which lists the books therein. For example, **Book Review Digest** of 1970 contains a reference to Saul Bellow's **Mr. Sammler's Planet** in

the index. In the body of **BRD** this title can be found under the author's last name. The reviews of Bellow's novel are drawn from over twenty periodicals, including **TLS, Yale Review, New Yorker, Library Journal, New York Times Book Review**, etc. In addition, three excerpts, ranging from 100 to 150 words, are quoted from reviews in **Book World, Harper's**, and the **New Republic**. When new editions of old books evoke reviews, these items appear also in **BRD**.

BRD indexes fairly popular reviewing media and, hence, often ignores scholarly works. While this publication can give one an idea of how some books were received, the specialized bibliographies and English journals will generally furnish material more pertinent to the serious scholar's purpose.

The New York Review of Books. Milford, Conn.: Milford Citizens Press, 1963-   [Irregularly; see below]

This publication reviews books in all subject areas, with a heavy concentration on literature; however, political material tends to be dominant. It has long review-articles as well as shorter review notices and also publishes some general essays and poems. **The New York Review** is distinguished by having many famous-name reviewers, and the reviews are usually stimulating, although often irritating and debatable; however, this is part of the periodical's appeal. It is published biweekly, except in July, August, September, and January, when it appears only once every three weeks.

Times Literary Supplement. London: **The Times**, 1902-   [Weekly]

This is a very comprehensive review of books in all fields. Long review-articles, shorter notices, essays, editorials, and letters to the editor are included. Traditionally, reviewers were always anonymous, but recently all reviews have been signed. **TLS** usually produces distinguished, thoughtful, well-researched, and well-written reviews.

BIBLIOGRAPHIES OF REVIEWS

Book Review Index. Detroit: Gale Research Company, 1965-   [Irregularly]

Although published irregularly, this scholarly tool has a yearly cumulation. It lists many more journals and has a much wider scope than the **Book Review Digest** but it does not annotate any entry. The author and book title are given, with full references (volume, date, page numbers) to the periodicals in which the reviews appeared. Unlike the **Book Review Digest**, this reference includes every book review in every periodical indexed. **Book Review Index** was suspended at the end of 1968, but publication was resumed in 1972. It will eventually be cumulated back to 1969.

An Index to Book Reviews in the Humanities. Williamston, Mich.: Phillip Thomson, 1960-   [Annually]

This work has yearly cumulations and itemized book reviews exclusively in the humanities (art and architecture, biography, drama and dance, folklore, history, language, literature, music, philosophy, and travel). It gives an impressively wide range of review sources and is especially useful because so many foreign journals are represented. It also includes reviews from many small and lesser-known American periodicals. No excerpts from the reviews themselves are given—just the location of each review.

At the front of each volume of the **Index** there is an identifying number given to each periodical in which reviews appear. **American Literature**, for instance, is designated by the number 27, while **Spectator** (London) is given the number 588. The reviews are listed alphabetically by author. If the periodical in which the review appears has a standard abbreviation, both the number and the abbreviation are given; e.g., "George Arms 27 (AL): Jan 66-488." If there is no standard abbreviation, then the number alone is given; e.g., "John Daniel, 588: 8 Jul 66-60." When in doubt about the periodical referred to, the reader must check the master list of numbers in the front of each volume.

6. Dissertations and Theses

In former years, only the graduate student was expected to examine doctoral dissertations, or theses, in order to gather in-depth information and to make certain that his or her research did not duplicate work already done. Now, as a result of much scholarly dedication and the advances made in microfilming and computer processing, dissertations (theses) are readily available to anyone who needs them.

McNamee's two volumes and **Dissertation Abstracts International**, listed directly below, furnish immediate and comprehensive data. The entries following those two are ranked in order of importance (as volumes with which researchers would presumably begin) rather than alphabetically or chronologically.

McNamee, Lawrence F., ed. **Dissertations in English and American Literature: Theses Accepted by American, British and German Universities 1865-1964.** New York: Bowker, 1968.

> This is a monumental work of scholarship—as comprehensive as its title indicates. It is also a tribute to the value of the computer in modern research because without machine help such a project would have taken many additional years to complete. A code number is listed for each subject as well as for each university from which a thesis originated. Thus, Joseph Conrad is numbered 1480, under which number the reader discovers the topics of dissertations written about Conrad, the author of each dissertation, its date, and the university which accepted it. There are extensive indexes to the code numbers, to the authors, and to the subjects (genre and chronological periods). This splendid volume should be the first checkpoint for anyone seeking information about dissertation topics. McNamee has also edited a **Supplement One** (New York: Bowker, 1969), which covers the period from 1964 to 1968.

49

Dissertation Abstracts International. Ann Arbor, Mich.: University Microfilms, 1938-   [Monthly]

From 1938 to 1951 this publication was entitled **Microfilm Abstracts.** In 1952 it became **Dissertation Abstracts: Abstracts of Dissertations and Monographs in Microform.** In July 1969 (volume 30) its name was changed again, to its present one, in order to include dissertations from universities outside the United States.

Issued monthly, and covering other fields in addition to language and literature, this publication prints a 250- to 500-word synopsis of the main points made in each doctoral dissertation listed. The dissertations are arranged alphabetically under subject. "Language and Literature" is the heading for English material. This heading is further subdivided into "General," "Classical," "Linguistics," and "Modern." In addition, the individual theses are alphabetized under each subheading by the writer's last name. The complete dissertation is available on microfilm and can be purchased directly from University Microfilms, Ann Arbor, Michigan. In most instances, the abstract will present enough information to determine whether the dissertation should be read in full. Of course, some graduate schools do not allow their dissertations to be abstracted, some have only recently granted such permission, and not all universities are involved in this program. Despite these factors, the abstracts—also available in printed form—are of immense help.

Starting with volume 27 (July 1966), **DA** was divided into separate issues: Humanities (A) and Sciences (B). Researchers will generally be led to materials in **DA** and **DAI** through the **MLA** bibliographies that commenced indexing **Dissertation Abstracts** in 1952.

Woodress, James L., **Dissertations in American Literature, 1891-1966.** Rev. and enl. ed. Durham, N.C.: Duke, 1968.

The first edition of this volume appeared in 1957 (covering 1891-1955) and a second edition was published in 1962 (with a supplement covering 1956-1961). The third and latest edition was published in 1968 and covers 1891-1966. This standard reference volume was originally issued well before McNamee's work. The entries indicate topic, author, and title of the dissertation, the university which accepted it, and the date of degree, e.g.,

HENRY JAMES
1446. Bockes, Douglas. The Late Method of HJ. Syracuse 54.

In addition to author headings, there are subject headings, e.g., "Drama," "Fiction," "General," "Folk Literature," "Transcendentalism." The Woodress volume is perhaps the most convenient source for those interested in American literature theses completed to the year 1966, but the McNamee volumes should also be consulted.

Altick, Richard D., and William R. Matthews, eds. **Guide to Doctoral Dissertations in Victorian Literature, 1886-1958.** Urbana: The University of Illinois Press, 1960.

Although now in great part superseded by the McNamee volumes, this book is still a convenient and quick guide for checking dissertation research in the Victorian period up to 1958. It is also still valuable because it includes French, Austrian, and Swiss dissertations, which are not covered by McNamee's volumes.

7. Biographies

There are countless excellent biographies of particular writers and allied literary figures, such as critics, but in this section we are concerned with significant general encyclopedic works that give fundamental data about many writers of various periods.

Allibone, S. Austin. **A Critical Dictionary of English Literature and British and American Authors, Living and Deceased, from the Earliest Accounts to the Middle of the Nineteenth Century**. 3 vols. Philadelphia: Childs and Peterson, and Lippincott, 1858. Reprint, Detroit: Gale Research Company, 1965.

Issued in three volumes, this reference treats the earliest writers, such as Bede and Chaucer, and then carries forward its biographies to the latter half of the nineteenth century. In 1891, Lippincott (Philadelphia) published John Foster Kirk's two-volume addition called **A Supplement to Allibone's Critical Dictionary**, which, however, covers only the period of approximately 1850-1888. Allibone's **Critical Dictionary** gives a brief biography or identification, lists the author's works, and then gives some critical excerpts about various works. Arranged alphabetically, its entries vary considerably in length. Some entries take only three or four lines, while others—depending primarily on the importance of the author—run to two or three pages. There are many worthwhile bibliographic references and some fine excerpts from book reviews of many authors' works. Allibone's volumes contain much unusual and little-known material and can lead to meaningful investigations and discoveries in books other than those of the writers it covers. Allibone is also especially informative about many of the lesser writers and critics. Much interesting and important data can be culled about authors such as Samuel Sewall, Lancelot Andrewes, Sir Thomas Overbury, Edmund Gosse, George Saintsbury, and Edward Bulwer-Lytton.

Biography Index: A Cumulative Index to Biographical Material in Books and Magazines. New York: H. W. Wilson, 1940-   [Quarterly]

This work lists biographical material in books and in over fifteen hundred periodicals. It gives references to individuals in all fields, not just literary personages. Published quarterly with annual cumulations, the main section is an alphabetical listing of individuals with references to biographical material about them. A second section arranges the individual names by profession and occupation.

Contemporary Authors: A Bio-bibliographical Guide to Current Authors and Their Works. Detroit: Gale Research Company, 1962-[Irregularly]

This is a most useful biographical reference compilation for present-day writers. Most of the entries are based on information given directly by the biographees—authors' comments on their writing, their future writing projects, their literary influences, etc. An unusually complete listing of their books is given as well as some address where they may be reached. **Contemporary Authors** is published irregularly, with cumulated indexes appearing usually every four years. As many as six volumes have been published annually.

It should be noted that **CA** tends to avoid the most well-known authors, e.g., Hemingway, Faulkner, and Frost, about whom much information is given in other reference works and critical studies. Much stress is placed on the minor and the up-and-coming literary figures.

Current Biography. New York: H. W. Wilson, 1940-   [Annually]

This reference gives biographical essays on prominent contemporary figures in all fields. It also adds a brief bibliography for each person discussed. It is especially valuable because it gives information on current writers that is sometimes difficult to find elsewhere. For example, essays appear on such contemporary talents as Allen Ginsberg, Joyce Carol Oates, Jerzy Grotowski, LeRoi Jones, James Dickey, Leonard Cohen, and Alexander Solzhenitsyn. The volumes are arranged alphabetically, and several of the issues have indexes for more than one year. There are also ten-year indexes: e.g., the 1960 volume indexes 1951-1960, and the 1970 yearbook has an index covering 1961-1970.

Dictionary of American Biography. 20 vols. New York: Scribner, 1928-1937.

The **DAB** first appeared in twenty volumes; later three supplements, one issued in 1944, another in 1958, and the most recent in 1973, were published. This work gives biographical material about famous deceased Americans in all fields of knowledge, although at times it appears to overemphasize political and government figures and not to present as complete a list as possible of literary personages. In instances where the **DAB** does comment on an author, e.g., Philip Freneau, it treats the materials with perception and gives useful, and sometimes obscure, bibliographical cross-references. For Freneau, the reader is directed to an article in the **Proceedings of the Huguenot Society of America**; for Emerson, there are references published in France and Germany. For completeness, the **DAB** materials should be supplemented by more recent studies of the authors discussed.

Dictionary of National Biography. 63 vols. London: Smith, Elder and Co.; New York: Macmillan, 1885-1900.

The most important biographical reference for important English figures who are deceased is the **DNB**. Arranged alphabetically by the biographee's last name, the original volumes were supplemented in 1901 by three additional tomes which included "accidental omissions from the previously published volumes" as well as individuals who died too late to be placed in the original work. The **DNB** was also printed (1901) in a different format that has twenty-one volumes and a supplement. Some libraries may have this issue. See also **Corrections and Additions to the Dictionary of National Biography** (Boston: G. K. Hall and Co., 1966) which appeared originally in various issues (from 1923 to 1903) of the Bulletin of the Institute of Historical Research (University of London).

Since its original publication, the **DNB** has been supplemented at roughly ten-year intervals—1901-1911; 1912-1921; 1922-1930, etc. The most recent issue, published by Oxford University Press in 1971, covers 1951-1960.

There is also available **The Concise Dictionary of National Biography**, which briefly epitomizes the principal facts in the **DND. Part 1: From the Beginning to 1900** was recently reprinted by Oxford University Press (1965), as was **Part 2: Being an** Epitome **of the** Twentieth Century DNB **Down to the End of 1950** (1961). Not only is the **DNB** especially notable for dealing thoroughly with essential biographical facts, but it also frequently gives data not found in other sources. Many of the cross-references found in the brief bibliographies at the end of the biographical essay are unusually valuable in that they give fresh and unusual insights and perspectives. For instance, in discussing Thomas Gray, the **DNB** remarks:

> Mason's **Life and Letters of Gray** (1774), in which the letters were connected on a plan said to have been suggested by Middleton's **Cicero**, was the first authority. Mason took astonishing liberties in altering and rearranging the letters. Johnson's **Life**, founded entirely on this, is the poorest in his series. . . . Mitford's edition of Gray's works, published by Pickering 1935-40, gave new letters and the correct text of those printed by Mason.

Such data are immensely valuable, both for succinctness and unusual information.

Kunitz, Stanley J. and Howard Haycraft, eds. **Twentieth Century Authors**. New York: H. W. Wilson, 1942.

This reference, arranged alphabetically, is an indispensable source of biographical information about authors who wrote during the first forty years of the present century. Some valuable critical information is also included. An additional volume, called **Twentieth Century Authors, First Supplement**, edited by Kunitz and Vineta Colby, was published in 1955 by H. W. Wilson. These two volumes base much of their data on information derived from questionnaires filled out by the authors themselves; consequently, much otherwise difficult-to-obtain or somewhat arcane data become available. Brief but generally useful bibliographies are given which direct the reader to many items which would otherwise not be recorded. In using the Kunitz volumes, one should begin with the 1942 volume and then read the 1955 supplement entry, since later biographical and literary details are given there. In some cases the material in the supplement has been rewritten to supersede the material in the 1942 edition, but even when this has occurred, one should still consult the original volume for information omitted in the rewritten supplement version: for instance, see the account of Liam O'Flaherty in both volumes.

Stanley Kunitz and Howard Haycraft edited three other volumes of particular interest to the English student, all of which were published by H. W. Wilson: **American Authors 1600-1900** (1938), **British Authors before 1800** (1952), and **British Authors of the Nineteenth Century** (1936).

These are all biographical reference guides that furnish concise, basic materials. While not as fresh and as revealing as Kunitz's two volumes on **Twentieth Century Authors**, primarily because no personal questionnaire was possible and many studies had already been written about these earlier authors, these books nevertheless have value for their readily accessible biographical information and critical estimates. A list of principal works and a brief bibliography of secondary studies is given for each writer. The books also serve as springboards for gathering more detailed and more recent materials.

Wakeman, John, ed. **World Authors 1950-1970**. New York: H. W. Wilson, 1975.

This compilation follows the format established by the Kunitz volumes. A biography is given, and critical analyses and bibliographies are provided. Sometimes the authors themselves have furnished additional comments. Also like the Kunitz volumes, this reference work is a convenient and informative point of departure for further study.

Who's Who. London: A. & C. Black, 1849-   [Annually]

This annual compilation includes brief entries about every important living British writer (as well as famous people in other fields) and presents additional recent information each year. Thus, when an author publishes a new novel or a collection of essays, this information will be added to his entry in the next edition. **Who's Who** is much less complete than the **DNB**, however, because it gives only brief data, e.g., place and date of birth, college attended, lists of literary works, dates of publication, etc.. This information is usually supplied to **Who's Who** by the author himself and is therefore only as accurate and as complete as the author wishes it to be. Some authors leave out significant facts, names of books they consider inferior, etc.; others give erroneous dates and titles, perhaps simply because memory plays tricks. Such undependability makes **Who's Who** a reference work to be checked against standard biographies and other sources.

Who's Who in America: A Biographical Dictionary of Notable Living Men and Women. Chicago: A. N. Marquis, 1900-   [Biennially]

The American counterpart of **Who's Who** is published once every two years. The entries are similar in content and format to the British volumes, giving the bare factual material of birth, education, publications, honors. Valuable in that it gives much essential and up-to-date information, it is nonetheless occasionally incomplete and inaccurate.

Who Was Who. London: A. & C. Black, 1916-   [Irregularly]

When a British author dies, his biographical entry is removed from **Who's Who** and placed in these volumes, with final details and date of death added. The volumes are supplemented frequently; for example, six volumes of **Who Was Who** have appeared to date: 1897-1915, 1916-1928, 1929-1940, 1941-1950, 1951-1960, and 1961-1970. If a researcher does not find the information he is seeking in **Who's Who** and is not certain if his authorial subject is still alive, he should check the volumes of **Who Was Who**.

Who Was Who in America. Chicago: A. N. Marquis, 1943- [Irregularly]

The same procedure used by the British is followed by the Americans when an important biographee from the United States dies. His entry is then transferred to **Who Was Who in America**. This volume appears at various intervals. The first publication covered 1897-1942, and the subsequent volumes have appeared irregularly, covering, for instance, 1943-1950, 1951-1960, etc.

8. Literary Histories

Literary histories give a unified, overall impression of such things as one period, or one genre, or one particular writer or school of writers. They also furnish helpful bibliographies, which are invariably in need of updating but do provide at least a starting point. Seeing the sweep of literature can also stimulate research ideas by suggesting areas or questions for further investigation.

ENGLISH LITERATURE

Baugh, Albert C., and others, eds. **A Literary History of England.** 2d ed. New York: Appleton-Century-Crofts, 1967.

> This is the best of the one-volume histories of English literature. Very detailed and with extensive footnotes, this book gives a valuable overall survey. Its only weak unit is the material covering the twentieth century up to 1939. Here it tends to overstress minor figures at the expense of major ones. Further, several important twentieth-century authors are not even mentioned. A number of the comments and analyses relating to writers of our century are woefully inadequate, e.g., the section on James Joyce. The volume includes an excellent bibliographical supplement which contains new data on all the periods covered.

Craig, Hardin, and others, eds. **A History of English Literature.** New York: Oxford, 1950. Reprint, New York: Collier Books, 1962.

> This is a pleasantly written and generally well-balanced survey but one not as detailed and as thoroughly documented as Baugh's **History** (preceding entry). The sections are written by different scholars; Louis Bredvold's account of the Restoration period and the eighteenth century is one of the outstanding units. The volume ends with a brief and inadequate commentary on Lawrence and Joyce.

Ward, A. W., and A. R. Waller, eds. **The Cambridge History of English Literature.** 15 vols. Cambridge, Engl.: Cambridge University Press, 1907-1927.

The Cambridge History is a very detailed survey of literature from the Anglo-Saxon period to the end of the nineteenth century. Each chapter is written by a specialist and provides generally sound and detailed—if at times outdated—evaluations. The volumes contain extensive bibliographies, which are now for the most part superseded. In addition to treating the major authors, The Cambridge History gives valuable information about minor writers, literary movements, and genres.

The volumes have been abridged to a one-volume edition which was also published by the Cambridge University Press but was edited by R. C. Churchill: The Concise Cambridge History of English Literature (3d rev. and enl. ed., 1969). Although this volume gives new data and adds material on the twentieth century, it is often sketchy and superficial; the comments are often unreliable and contain several questionable generalizations and views.

Wilson, Frank P., Bonamy Dobrée, and Norman Davis, eds. **Oxford History of English Literature.** Oxford: Clarendon Press, 1945- [Irregularly]

This is an ongoing series of volumes, each written by a single author. All the works are extremely scholarly and thorough and provide comprehensive bibliographies. Since most of the volumes have been written relatively recently, they have an especially fresh appeal. The following **OHEL** series list indicates both already published, as well as forthcoming, volumes:

Vol. 1. **Part 1.** J. C. Pope. **English Literature before the Norman Conquest** (to be published).
Part 2. J. A. W. Bennett. **Middle English Literature** (to be published).
Vol. 2. **Part 1.** Henry S. Bennett. **Chaucer and the Fifteenth Century.** Oxford: Clarendon Press, 1947.
Part 2. Edmund K. Chambers. **English Literature at the Close of the Middle Ages.** Oxford: Clarendon Press, 1945.
Vol. 3. C. S. Lewis. **English Literature in the Sixteenth Century (excluding Drama).** Oxford: Clarendon Press, 1954.
Vol. 4. **Part 1.** F. P. Wilson and G. K. Hunter. **The English Drama, 1485-1585.** New York: Oxford University Press, 1969.
Part 2. Alfred Harbage. **The English Drama c. 1586-1642** (to be published).
Vol. 5. Douglas Bush. **English Literature in the Earlier Seventeenth Century, 1600-1660.** 2d ed. rev. Oxford: Clarendon Press, 1962.

Vol. 6.   James   Sutherland. **English Literature of the Late Seventeenth Century.** New York: Oxford University Press, 1969.
Vol. 7.   Bonamy Dobrée. **English Literature in the Early Eighteenth Century.** Oxford: Clarendon Press, 1959.
Vol. 8.   John Butt. **The Mid-Eighteenth Century** (to be published).
Vol. 9.   W. L. Renwick. **English Literature, 1789-1815.** Oxford: Clarendon Press, 1963.
Vol. 10.   Ian Jack. **English Literature, 1815-1832.** Oxford: Clarendon Press, 1963.
Vol. 11.   Geoffrey and Kathleen Tillotson. **The Mid-Nineteenth Century** (to be published).
Vol. 12.   John I. M. Stewart. **Eight Modern Writers.** Oxford: Clarendon Press, 1963. The writers analyzed are Hardy, James, Shaw, Conrad, Kipling, Yeats, Joyce, and Lawrence.

AMERICAN LITERATURE

Quinn, Arthur Hobson. **The Literature of the American People, An Historical and Critical Survey.** New York: Appleton-Century-Crofts, 1951.

It must be readily admitted that no volume now rivals Spiller's **Literary History of the United States**, yet researchers might profit by examining Quinn's survey, which extends from the earliest writing up to the beginning of the World War II era. There are extensive bibliographies of all periods of literature, of movements, and of individual writers, although these checklists must be supplemented by Spiller, the **MLA Bibliography**, etc.
Quinn handles his material by relating literature to historical, political, and artistic characteristics of each period. He is overly zealous in his viewing of literature as being continually interrelated with other aspects of American life, and many interpretations are dated and lack scholarly support. At the same time, he conveys numerous stimulating and thought-provoking ideas and theories.

Spiller, Robert E., and others, eds. **Literary History of the United States.** 4th ed. rev. New York: Macmillan, 1974.

The sections of Spiller's **Literary History** have been written by various specialists and present well-researched and detailed accounts of the history of American literature. This work is now the most respected and most frequently consulted American literary history. It has the benefits of contemporary scholarship and contains the most extensive bibliographies of individual American writers yet compiled, as well as very thorough checklists on movements and influences and allied subjects. It is an indispensable reference and research tool. The first volume, **History**, has a selective general bibliography at the end; the second volume, **Bibliography**, is devoted exclusively to exactly that.

Since researchers may encounter this **LHUS Bibliography** in some other form than that of the fourth edition revised, some knowledge of its earlier publishing history is appropriate. The bibliography unit, edited by Thomas H. Johnson, was originally published by Macmillan in 1948, and a supplementary bibliography, edited by Richard Ludwig, was issued in 1959. These two extensive checklists were combined in one volume in 1963, and in 1972 another supplement appeared. These various units, revised and updated, have now been combined in the one-volume 1974 edition.

Trent, William P., and others, eds. **The Cambridge History of American Literature.** 3 vols. New York: Macmillan, 1933.

This is an account of America's literature from the earliest period to the very early part of the twentieth century. The volumes discuss authors, literary trends and movements, as well as historical connections. They also supply very detailed bibliographies which must now be updated. Some of the views expressed are out of fashion and incomplete because of new research and study, but the books are still highly useful, particularly for their coverage of the earlier periods. A one-volume edition was published by Macmillan in 1943 and reprinted in 1967.

9. Surveys of Literary Criticism

Although there are many available compendiums of literary criticism, the immediately following volume is both scholarly and pleasant to read. The works listed thereafter are among the most readable and useful for the student of English and American literature.

GENERAL

Wimsatt, William K., and Cleanth Brooks. **Literary Criticism: A Short History**. New York: Knopf, 1957.

It is difficult to conceive of a better one-volume survey of literary criticism. This book includes studies of Greek and Roman classicism, of criticism in the Renaissance and during the Augustan, Romantic, and Victorian eras, and of British and American criticism during the twentieth-century. It treats both movements and individual figures. Among the ancient critics analyzed are Aristotle, Plato, Horace, Longinus; and among the moderns, I. A. Richards, Eliot, and Pound. This work deserves its reputation of being very scholarly and extremely perceptive, although it has also evoked some controversy. There are extensive footnotes as well as a brief bibliography at the beginning of the book.

ENGLISH

Atkins, John W. H. **English Literary Criticism: The Medieval Phase.** New York: Macmillan, 1943.

This work surveys the criticism of the Middle English period. Atkins' approach is primarily descriptive. He takes the documents, then summarizes, or reports, and draws the obvious conclusions. His work is far from complete or definitive. Since 1943 new interpretations of critical material have been formulated, and there are also new ways of defining what is critical (e.g., Chaucer's critical principles are found within his creative work).

Atkins, John W. H. **English Literary Criticism: The Renascence**. 2d ed. London: Methuen, 1951.

This survey covers the period 1500-1650. It studies the beginnings of dramatic criticism in England, shows the effect of humanism, and notes critical theories on prose and poetry. The book is especially good in calling attention to the minor figures. A useful volume that helps to clarify the main critical concepts and movements, it must nevertheless be supplemented by the results of more recent scholarship.

Atkins, John W. H. **English Literary Criticism: Seventeenth and Eighteenth Centuries**. London: Methuen, 1951.

Atkins examines French and English neoclassicism and reviews the attitudes toward drama and poetry. Extensive treatment is given the views of Samuel Johnson. A worthwhile chapter considers Shakespearean criticism in the seventeenth and eighteenth centuries.

In all his works, Atkins gives a helpful overall picture of literary criticism which most researchers will find indispensable. It is true that at times he oversimplifies or misses the subtleties and fine points, but such particulars will be observed only by specialists. In any case, the Atkins' histories should be checked with the discoveries of the latest research.

Wellek, René. **A History of Modern Criticism, 1750-1950**. New Haven: Yale University Press, 1955-

This study will comprise five volumes, four of which have already appeared. Two, **The Later Eighteenth Century**, and **The Romantic Age**, were published in 1955, and two, **The Age of Transition**, and **The Later Nineteenth Century**, in 1965. The fifth volume, still to come, will be devoted to the twentieth century.

Wellek concentrates on various movements and the critical giants of each era. Such authors as Voltaire, Diderot, and Johnson are studied in connection with neoclassicism. Goethe, Kant, and Schiller are analyzed as part of the German "Sturm und Drang" era. The work is international in scope; e.g., Romanticism is discussed as it appears in Germany and Italy as well as in England. In addition to far-ranging scope and in-depth analyses, the books are distinguished by extensive bibliographies. This is a work of amazing erudition and value, and the volumes published so far are among the monumental works in the field of literature. While lauding Wellek's achievement, it must be pointed out that many scholars consider some of his ideas controversial. Certainly he is guilty at times of preconceptions and also has his critical blind spots.

AMERICAN

Glicksberg, Charles. **American Literary Criticism 1900-1950.** New York: Hendricks House, 1951.

This is a useful commentary on the writings of the most significant modern American literary critics. Among the critics analyzed are Edmund Wilson, Lionel Trilling, Yvor Winters, Allen Tate, Paul Elmer More, Irving Babbitt, and Kenneth Burke. Glicksberg presents a brief biography of each figure, surveys his writings and ideas, gives a bibliography, and prints one or two essays typical of the critic's point of view. This is a convenient introduction to the chief American critics of the early half of our century.*

Stovall, Floyd, ed. **The Development of American Literary Criticism.** Chapel Hill: The University of North Carolina Press, 1955.

Stovall's work surveys American criticism beginning in the 1800s and continuing to the early 1950s. It is a generally sound and informative overview, mentioning the important developments, writings, etc. C. Hugh Holman contributes an especially effective essay on "The Defense of Art: Criticism since 1930." Stovall also gives an excellent reading list.*

*Both the Glicksberg and the Stovall volumes must be supplemented by Wimsatt and Brooks (see beginning of chapter) and by later materials listed in standard bibliographies such as **MLA** and **MHRA**.

10. *Irish, Australian, and Canadian Materials*

IRISH MATERIALS

Material for research on Irish authors can be found in the standard English references mentioned in this book; for example, the **NCBEL** lists essential bibliography on Joyce, O'Casey, O'Faolain, and other important Irish figures. Two other particularly useful bibliographies are the following.

Harmon, Maurice. **Modern Irish Literature 1800-1967: A Reader's Guide**. Chester Springs, Pa.: Dufour Editions, 1968.

> Harmon presents some of the basic works relating to every aspect of Irish life—political, social, literary, etc. Although this study is often too brief and omits important material, it at least gives the reader an opportunity to become aware of several significant studies, e.g., criticism like Thomas Flanagan's **The Irish Novelists, 1800-1850** and Benedict Kiely's **Modern Irish Fiction—A Critique**, and anthologies such as Kathleen Hoagland's **1000 Years of Irish Poetry**.

Mikhail, E. H. **A Bibliography of Modern Irish Drama 1899-1970**. Seattle: University of Washington Press, 1972.

> This is an extremely concise checklist of bibliographies containing material about the Irish theater. Mikhail also gives a listing of books, periodical articles, and unpublished materials about the topic, although he omits much significant primary material for which the **NCBEL** and other standard reference works should be consulted.

AUSTRALIAN AND CANADIAN MATERIALS

Australian and Canadian material have their own reference sources, although the **MLA International Bibliography** lists many Canadian ones. The following bibliographies are among the most useful.

"Annual Bibliography of Commonwealth Literature," in **Journal of Commonwealth Literature**, 1964-   [Annually]

> Each December since 1965 this compilation has appeared in the **Journal** (which has editorial offices at the University of Leeds [England] but is published by Oxford University Press). The bibliography lists books by, and studies of, authors as well as periodical material found in Canada, Australia, and other British Commonwealth nations.

"Canadian Literature: A Checklist," in **Canadian Literature**, 1959- [Annually]

> This checklist (published by the University of British Columbia, Vancouver) has appeared each year since 1960 and lists books and articles covering all genres of literature.

Canadian Periodical Index. Toronto, later Ottawa: now issued by the Canadian Library Association, 1948- [Monthly; annual cumulation]

> This index (both author and subject) covers the most popular and significant journals in Canada. A particularly useful reference tool, it is well-printed and convenient to use. It is also more readily accessible in American public and university libraries than the two previously mentioned entries.

Dutton, Geoffrey, ed. **The Literature of Australia**. Middlesex, Engl.: Penguin Books, 1964.

> A survey of the more important Australian writers, Dutton's book is notable for several perceptive essays by knowledgeable literary experts as well as for basic bibliography by and about the writers themselves. The book also provides bibliography of cultural, social, and intellectual background.

Green, H. M. **A History of Australian Literature, Pure and Applied**. 2 vols. Sydney: Angus & Robertson, Ltd., 1961.

> Green himself furnishes an apt description of his work: "A critical review of all forms of literature produced in Australia from the first books published after the arrival of the First Fleet until 1950, with short accounts of later publications up to 1960." This is a far-reaching survey of all aspects of Australian writing. Although it covers a wider range of material than Dutton's work and is invaluable, it is deficient in bibliography, and the American student of literature will find Dutton much more helpful.

Klinck, Carl F., and others, eds. **Literary History of Canada: Canadian Literature in English**. Toronto: University of Toronto Press, 1965.

This is an indispensable guide to all aspects of Canadian writing, including essays, scientific work, travel books, philosophical treatises, as well as fiction and poetry. It examines the origins and development of Canadian writing, emphasizing the most significant figures. Klinck's study also includes an extensive bibliography of considerable value.

11. *Historical Surveys of the Novel*

The amount of historical and critical material concerning the novel is vast and can be confusing, but several surveys help to bring about some order and to put the pieces of the larger picture into place. In addition to the best-known guides, the supplementary data found in recent bibliographies, and especially in the following books, will help considerably in presenting an overall view.

THE ENGLISH NOVEL

Allen, Walter. **The English Novel: A Short Critical History**. New York: Dutton, 1954.

> This one-volume study is a generally judicious survey from the earliest period of writing to 1914. There is a short section on writers after 1914, but it is totally inadequate. Whereas Allen's commentary is at times far from faultless and his work lacks bibliographical material, he provides a valuable, concise overview—particularly of the eighteenth- and nineteenth-century British novel.

Baker, Ernest A. **The History of the English Novel**. 10 vols. London: Witherby, Ltd., 1924-1939. Reprint, New York: Barnes & Noble, 1950-1961.

> This is the lengthiest study of British fiction ever written, covering the beginnings of prose fiction in the age of romance and continuing to such writers as Conrad, Kipling, Galsworthy, and Lawrence. It is extremely dated, and tends to be descriptive with much plot summary. It needs to be supplemented by more penetrating and more recent critical and analytical works. While the ten volumes contain considerable bibliographical material both on periods and on individual authors, these lists need to be supplemented by other more up-to-date works.

Stevenson, Lionel. **The English Novel: A Panorama**. Boston: Houghton Mifflin, 1960.

This is an excellent one-volume survey that starts with the pastoral, picaresque, allegorical, and similar genres and carries along well to such moderns as Joyce, Woolf, and Lawrence. Stevenson's comments are generally balanced, thoughtful, and reasonable. The book is sketchy and unsatisfactory on writers since the 1940s. The bibliography is relatively brief, but the selections are carefully chosen.

Wagenknecht, Edward. **Cavalcade of the English Novel**. New York: Holt, 1954.

First published in 1943, this volume had a supplementary bibliography added to it for its 1954 printing. Although it is a readable, informative, and well-organized study, it is sometimes marred by facile observations, unnecessary sketchiness, and questionable generalizations. Nevertheless, it is a pleasant introduction to its subject and a useful road map. It contains much concise, worthwhile data on minor novelists. The supplementary bibliography, while quite extensive, needs to be supported by more recent research.

THE ENGLISH AND AMERICAN NOVEL

Allen, Walter. **The Modern Novel in Britain and the United States**. New York: Dutton, 1964.

Allen considers the novel during the twenties and thirties and deals with World War II and postwar eras. While he does not supply bibliographies, Allen provides a sensitive overall approach—a survey introduction, to be sure, but a generally sound one. His work must be supplemented by other books and articles. He takes the reader to the work of such contemporary figures as Angus Wilson, Iris Murdoch, William Golding, Flannery O'Connor, and J. D. Salinger; but material on these writers is much less thorough than that given for the writers of the 1920s and 1930s.

THE AMERICAN NOVEL

In dealing with the twentieth-century American novel, many critical studies must be consulted. The critiques of Joseph Warren Beach, Maxwell Geismar, Leon Edel, and Ihab Hassan—to mention just a few—are mandatory reading; the MLA bibliographies and the bibliographies in Spiller's **Literary History** will provide further direction. Some of the basic introductory materials are listed here.

Cowie, Alexander. **The Rise of the American Novel**. New York: American Book, 1948.

Cowie presents an excellent view of the beginnings of American fiction. He gives major emphasis to Cooper, Hawthorne, Melville, Twain, Howells, and James; but with the possible exceptions of Cooper, Hawthorne, and Howells, his work on these principal novelists needs to be qualified with more recent knowledge and interpretations. He is especially informative about the minor figures of the eighteenth and nineteenth centuries.

Hoffman, Frederick J. **The Modern Novel in America**. Chicago: Regnery, 1951.

This short volume covers the period from 1900 to 1950. Although there are several gaps in this book, and it is often disappointingly superficial, it provides a good, quick survey of main trends and principal authors. While it must be supplemented by additional sources, it furnishes one with a bird's-eye view that is often needed in an area so vast.

Quinn, Arthur H. **American Fiction: An Historical and Critical Survey**. New York: Appleton-Century, 1936.

Studying the novel and the short story from the earliest era of American writing to the 1930s, Quinn offers mainly descriptive, and some critical, material dealing with the major and minor authors. He is highly inadequate in dealing with the twentieth century; and overall, many of his views are outdated, superficial, and must often be qualified. He does write well, however, and supplies guideposts through territory that previously had not been clearly charted. His bibliographies badly need updating.

Wagenknecht, Edward. **Cavalcade of the American Novel**. New York: Holt, 1952.

This volume is a companion piece to Wagenknecht's **Cavalcade of the English Novel**, cited earlier in this chapter. The comments given with that entry apply here also. Highly pleasant reading with generalizations which must be constantly challenged, this work nevertheless furnishes an interesting—if often facile—overview for one to examine before turning to the deeper strata of more perplexing and more difficult problems and questions. The bibliographies must be supplemented with more recent material.

12. *Basic Drama Materials*

The subject of drama includes an immense body of material. The books discussed on the following pages concentrate on significant, fundamental topics; their references and bibliographies will lead the reader to additional material.

BIBLIOGRAPHY

Faxon, Frederick W., and others, eds. **Cumulated Dramatic Index, 1909-1949.** 2 vols. Boston: G. K. Hall and Co., 1965.

This is an index to the forty-one annual volumes of the **Dramatic Index** published by F. W. Faxon Company from 1909 to 1949. (Faxon was both a compiler, or editor, and a publisher.) The **Dramatic Index** had been published in the quarterly issues of the **Bulletin of Bibliography.** It is a very useful index for the time covered, since it lists not only materials about playwrights (American, some British, a few Irish) and drama theory but also includes references to actors, reviews, and almost all other aspects of the theater. Above all, it presents much basic information about the plays themselves (including revivals).

"Modern Drama: A Selective Bibliography of Works Published in English," in **Modern Drama,** 1958-   [Annually]

From 1960 to 1968, **Modern Drama** (see Chapter 19) published a bibliography of materials concerned with twentieth-century drama. Drama items about non-English speaking countries are included, making this an indispensable checklist. **MD** has recommenced publication of the annual bibliography in its March 1974 (volume 17) number. This issue covers material published in 1972 and 1973. The next bibliography listing will focus on 1974.

Stratman, Carl. **Bibliography of Medieval Drama.** Berkeley: University of California Press, 1954.

Stratman lists individual plays, play cycles, and individual dramatists, such as Hrotsvitha. Useful information is given about various editions and collections in which the text of these plays may be found. In addition to treating English drama, this book has sections on French, Latin, German, Byzantine, Italian, and Spanish drama. It also notes masters' theses and doctoral dissertations. While it must be supplemented by more recent bibliographies, this work has become a central starting point for serious studies of medieval drama.

Wells, Stanley, ed. **English Drama (excluding Shakespeare).** London: Oxford University Press, 1975.

Another of the Oxford Select Bibliographical Guides, this volume attempts to point out the best editions, biographies, critical studies, and background materials in the field of British drama from the medieval period to the present day. Although the essays on the earlier periods are especially informative, the sections dealing with twentieth-century plays are often sketchy. Perhaps the scholars were hampered by editorially imposed space limitations.

HANDBOOKS AND DIRECTORIES

Anderson, Michael, Jacques Guicharnaud, and others, eds. **Crowell's Handbook of Contemporary Drama.** New York: Thomas Y. Crowell, 1971.

Alphabetically arranged, this handbook is concerned with theatrical developments, playwrights, and significant plays. It deals with drama in all countries since World War II and gives biographies of playwrights, comments on their writing, and describes the content of many plays. It also discusses special terms, movements, and theories, as well as important theater companies and directors. This is the best reference guide for post-World War II drama.

Hartnoll, Phyllis, ed. **Oxford Companion to the Theatre.** 3d ed. London: Oxford University Press, 1967.

This is more Continental in emphasis and more thorough than Sobel's **New Theatre Handbook and Digest of Plays,** but Sobel's work does add several items not found in the **Oxford Companion.** The **Companion** surveys the history of theater in theatrically important countries and contains units on famous actors and playwrights. It does not give plot summaries or critical comments about famous plays, but it does cover an impressive range of subject matter. Among the subjects mentioned are harlequinade, cothurnus, stichomythia, fate drama, Max Reinhardt, multiple setting, Accius, Provincetown Players, and Victorien Sardou.

McGraw-Hill Encyclopedia of World Drama. 4 vols. New York: McGraw-Hill, 1972.

This work is a wide-ranging compilation of data relating to the theater. It lists all plays of the world's principal playwrights, gives significant dates, biographical material, synopses, and critiques. The volumes are heavily and attractively illustrated.

Parker, John [orig. comp.], **Who's Who in the Theatre**. 15th ed. New York: Pitman, 1972.

First published and edited by John Parker in 1912, this useful reference presents detailed biographies of living dramatists of all countries, focusing on the significant data and offering an especially detailed list of each writer's works. It also gives biographies of actors, actresses, producers, and others associated with the theater. It lists Shakespeare's plays performed at the Old Vic, as well as other notable productions and important revivals.

Shipley, Joseph T. **Guide to Great Plays**. Washington, D. C.: Public Affairs Press, 1956.

Shipley discusses significant plays by authors of all countries. He gives the background of the drama, some plot summaries, and critical comments by reviewers and critics. He indicates the importance of each play as well as the dates of its initial run. Shipley's approach is primarily one of easygoing description rather than critical analysis; nevertheless, he does bring together in one volume a considerable amount of informative data.

Sobel, Bernard. **The New Theatre Handbook and Digest of Plays**. New York: Crown, 1959.

Sobel gives commentary about authors, individual plays, principal dates of theater interest, technical and general terms, and similar materials relating to the drama. (See also the comments under Hartnoll's **Oxford Companion**, mentioned earlier in this chapter.) Some sample entries are Korean drama, **Hannele**, impressionism, George Pierce Baker, psychoanalysis in the drama, Leonid Andreyev, poetic drama, "gagging," and **The Sea Gull**.

HISTORIES—GENERAL

Clark, Barrett, and George Freedley, eds. **A History of Modern Drama**. New York: Appleton-Century, 1947.

Clark and Freedley is a very thorough and perceptive survey of drama in the late nineteenth and the twentieth centuries. It discusses the drama of almost every notable country in the world. For example, it deals with South American, modern Greek, and Yiddish and Hebrew drama. A bibliography on the drama of each country is also given.

Nicoll, Allardyce. **English Drama, 1900-1930: The Beginnings of the Modern Period**. Cambridge, Engl.: Cambridge University Press, 1973.

This work, a continuation of Nicoll's six-volume history of drama from 1660 to 1900, surveys the basic movements and major and minor playwrights of the period from 1900 to 1930. It presents a detailed list of plays published and performed in the British Isles.

Nicoll, Allardyce. **A History of English Drama, 1660-1900**. 6 vols. Cambridge, Engl.: Cambridge University Press, 1952-1959.

The first five volumes survey English drama from the Restoration to the end of the nineteenth century. The sixth volume consists of and is subtitled, **A Short-titled Alphabetical Catalogue of Plays Produced or Printed in England from 1600 to 1900.**
    Nicoll's observations are sometimes too facile and oversimplified; his history must, therefore, be supported by other materials. He has, nevertheless, a highly readable style and gives a coherent panoramic view which researchers will find handy. This study is much more leisurely and rambling than his commentary on world drama. (See following entry.)

Nicoll, Allardyce. **World Drama from Aeschylus to Anouilh**. London: Harrap, 1949.

This study surveys drama from the time of the Greeks and the Romans, through its developments in England, Italy, France, Spain, and Germany, and up to the 1940s. Nicoll examines such diverse subjects as the commedia dell' arte, French romanticism and classicism, the Spanish stage of Lope de Vega and Calderón, and the nineteenth-century Russian theater. He even devotes a section to Sanskrit, Chinese, and Japanese drama. The very nature of this study forces it to be rather superficial, but it is well written and very informative and gives one a fundamental acquaintance with the history of world drama.

HISTORIES—SPECIFIC PERIODS

The books in this listing are arranged chronologically according to the period they analyze.

Chambers, E. K. **The Medieval Stage**. 2 vols. London: Oxford University Press, 1903.

This work is a monumental study of medieval theater. Chambers discusses in detail minstrelsy, folk drama, festival plays, liturgical and secularized guild plays, pageants, puppet plays, interludes, etc. He provides thorough footnotes and a bibliography on all topics. In the appendixes, Chambers publishes material from various account books and from minstrel guilds and even deals with such items as sword dances and the Coventry Hock-Tuesday Show. While additional twentieth-century research must supplement Chambers's materials, his book remains a rich storehouse of information.

Young, Karl. **The Drama of the Medieval Church**. 2 vols. Oxford: Clarendon Press, 1933.

The classic commentary on church drama, this intensely scholarly study explains in detail the origins and backgrounds of religious plays and publishes the texts of extant church dramas. The texts are supplemented with detailed notes and explanations.

Chambers, E. K. **The Elizabethan Stage**. 4 vols. Oxford: Clarendon Press, 1923. Reprint, with corrections, 1951.

Chambers deals with the period from 1558 to 1616. He studies the mask, the court play, the effects of humanism and Puritanism, the adult and boy companies of actors, the public and private theaters, staging, the playwrights, the printing of the plays, and similar subjects. It is difficult to imagine any aspect of Elizabethan drama which Chambers has ignored. Although modern scholarship may add details, interpretations, and new insights, it is building on a firm and thorough foundation supplied in these volumes.

Bentley, Gerald. **The Jacobean and Caroline Stage**. 7 vols. Oxford: Clarendon Press, 1941-1968.

Covering the years 1616 to 1642, this work is a continuation of Chambers's volumes and is a classic research study in its own right. Bentley presents a thorough history of the London dramatic companies with such details as actor lists, provincial notes, plays at court, and repertory. He gives every bit of information possible about the actors of this period and discusses the plays and playwrights and the situation of the theater in general. Volume 7 has appendixes and a general index to all volumes.

The London Stage 1660-1800: A Calendar of Plays, Entertainments and Afterpieces together with Casts, Box-Receipts and Contemporary Comment, Compiled from the Playbills, Newspapers and Theatrical Diaries of the Period. Carbondale: Southern Illinois University Press, 1960-1968.

Aptly described by its subtitle, this is a very specialized study composed mostly of lists. The general introductions to each part are, however, extremely informative, and even nonspecialists will find them of considerable value. This collection has been issued in five parts.

Part 1.   William Van Lennep, ed. **1660-1700.** 1965.
Part 2.   Emmett L. Avery, ed. **1700-1729.** 2 vols. 1960.
Part 3.   Arthur H. Scouten, ed. **1729-1747.** 2 vols. 1961.
Part 4.   George Winchester Stone, ed. **1747-1776.** 3 vols. 1962.
Part 5.   Charles Beecher Hogan, ed. **1776-1800.** 3 vols. 1968.

Rowell, George. **The Victorian Theatre, A Survey**. New York: Oxford University Press, 1956.

This commentary covers the period from 1792 to 1914. Rowell maintains that influences on the Victorian drama can be traced back to 1792. He gives an effective survey but omits comment on closet dramas by significant writers, such as Tennyson and Browning. A play list for the era is included as well as a detailed bibliography.

DRAMA PERIODICALS

The journal **Modern Drama** is mentioned earlier in this chapter and also in Chapter 19. Two other important journals are listed below.

The Drama Review, 1955-   [Quarterly]

With its Fall 1967 issue (volume 12), the title of this periodical was changed from **Tulane Drama Review** to the present title and the editorial offices were moved from Tulane University to New York

University. The **Review** has traditionally been one of the most scholarly and informative sources in the field of drama. It has published important issues devoted to particular playwrights (e.g., a Summer 1959 Jean Giraudoux number) and has also produced valuable bibliographies (e.g., a Christopher Fry checklist in the Spring 1960 number). In recent years the **Review** has given itself to avant-garde theater and has chronicled and encouraged experimental and revolutionary theater. It is the leading periodical handling such material.

Educational Theatre Journal, 1949-   [Quarterly]

This periodical reviews plays and books, comments on theater activities throughout the world, and prints articles of scholarship and criticism in theater arts. Some typical articles are "The Critical Reception of Eugene O'Neill on the French Stage," "**Tamburlaine** for the Modern Stage," and "**The Plough and the Stars**—The Destructive Consequences of Human Folly."

SHAKESPEARE

As is well known, more books have been written about Shakespeare than about any other literary figure. From this voluminous amount of material, I have selected a few basic studies that are important in themselves and that are also good guides to additional works about Shakespeare. Obviously, the annual bibliography in the **Shakespeare Quarterly**, described in Chapter 3, must be mentioned again. Readers are also referred to the Tannenbaum **Elizabethan Bibliographies** discussed in Chapter 2.

Bullough, Geoffrey, ed. **Narrative and Dramatic Sources of Shakespeare**. 8 vols. New York: Columbia, 1957-1975.

These volumes are indispensable works of scholarship. Bullough speaks at length about the sources of Shakespeare's plays and then gives in full the various source passages and probable source passages and analogues. He also presents a critical bibliography for the sources of each of the plays.

Campbell, Oscar J., ed. **The Reader's Encyclopedia of Shakespeare**. New York: Thomas Y. Crowell, 1966.

This is a compilation of a vast amount of data about Shakespeare's life and writing, and since it has been published fairly recently it contains much current data. It comments on the dates and sources of the plays, gives the known biographical facts, supplies critical views, and, in general, serves as a concise Shakespeare encyclopedia.

Chambers, E. K. **William Shakespeare: A Study of Facts and Problems**. 2 vols. Oxford: Clarendon Press, 1930.

Chambers intended this study to be a companion to his **Elizabethan Stage** because he could not deal adequately with Shakespeare in that work. He records facts about Shakespeare and his company, the quartos and the first folio, the problems of authenticity, and matters of a related nature. He deals with specialized aspects of Shakespeare's life and career and comments on such issues as the coat of arms, the marriage certificate, lawsuits, the will, and even the epitaphs. Chambers presents a valuable compendium; and although modern scholarship adds further data and interpretations, this book remains a standard reference.

Ebisch, Walter, and Levin Schücking. **A Shakespeare Bibliography**. Oxford: Clarendon Press, 1931.

This is a selected bibliography of articles about Shakespeare, in books and journals, which runs to the year 1929. The bibliography concerns itself with all phases of its subject—Shakespeare's life, his texts and sources, apocrypha, productions of his plays, etc. There are sections dealing with his attitude toward the state, the law, science, art, education, the supernatural, social classes, etc. A **Supplement for the years 1930-1935** was issued by the Clarendon Press in 1937, and G. R. Smith continued the work of Ebisch and Schücking in his **A Classified Shakespeare Bibliography, 1936-1958** (University Park, Pa.: Pennsylvania State University Press, 1963). The Smith volume supplies essential bibliographical material.

Ralli, Augustus. **A History of Shakespearian Criticism**. 2 vols. Oxford: Oxford University Press, 1932. Reprint, New York: Humanities Press, 1959.

Starting from Shakespeare's time and carrying his data to 1925, Ralli presents a summary of what the important critics have said about Shakespeare. The volumes cover literary critiques in France and Germany as well as in England. For a survey, this work is very thorough, and although it misses several critical subtleties, it furnishes readers with a convenient historical view of the main trends in Shakespeare analysis.

Shakespeare Survey, 1948-   [Annually]

This survey of Shakespearian study and production contains essays on various phases of Shakespeare with emphasis on what the last fifty years have contributed to the study. Some of the principal articles in the **Survey** have titles like "Fifty Years of the Criticism of Shakespeare's Style," "Studies in **Hamlet** 1901-1955." and "Shakespeare's Romances: 1900-1957." Some of the volumes are built around one topic, e.g., **King Lear**, or the poems and music. In addition, a yearly survey of current Shakespeare scholarship (see Index for references) is published. The **Shakespeare Survey** is mandatory reading for those interested in Shakespeare's drama.

Thomson, W. H. **Shakespeare's Characters: A Historical Dictionary**. New York: British Book Centre, 1951.

This is a dictionary of all historical personages appearing as characters in, or mentioned in, Shakespeare's English history plays and **Macbeth**. It gives a biography of each character as well as a list of the plays in which the character appears. It also analyzes various dynasties, the Houses of Lancaster, York, Percy, Plantagenet, etc., and explains the claims of Henry IV to the English throne and of Henry V to the French crown. Thomson's work helps one to understand Shakespeare's history plays more fully.

Wells, Stanley, ed. **Shakespeare**. London: Oxford University Press, 1973.

This volume in the Select Bibliographical Guides series is designed to direct readers to "the best in Shakespeare scholarship and criticism." Each chapter is written by a different scholar. In addition to the individual plays, subjects covered include Shakespeare's text, the sonnets and other poems, and general background, such as biography, sources and influences, and historical, social, and philosophical aspects. This book furnishes a worthwhile introduction to basic Shakespearean materials.

13. Basic Ballad Materials

The modern use of ballads for social and political protest has not only brought attention to the contemporary folk-style ballads of such composers as Pete Seeger, Bob Dylan, Arlo Guthrie, etc., but has increased awareness of the old ballads, which have always been discussed in introductory literature and English courses. Today it is not unusual to hear ballads such as "Bonnie Barbara Allen," "The Twa Corbies," or "Hind Horn" sung and discussed apart from formal courses.

Aside from the classic Child's, which is mentioned first, there are four books that are especially good for acquainting one with fundamental information and background about the old folk songs.

Child, Francis J., ed. **The English and Scottish Popular Ballads**. 5 vols. Boston: Houghton Mifflin, 1882-1898. Reprint, New York: Cooper Square Publishers, 1962.

> This is the classic collection of traditional ballads. Child prints the text of over three hundred ballads and also gives their various versions. Thus, fifteen versions of "Lord Randal" are listed, and eighteen readings of "Sir Patrick Spens." Child also furnishes introductions to, and commentary about, what is known of ballad origins, dates, variations, and allied matters. He explains the meanings of words and phrases both in footnotes and in the glossary in volume 5. Volume 5 also indexes the materials and provides a detailed bibliography.

Bronson, Bertrand H., ed. **The Traditional Tunes of the Child Ballads**. 4 vols. Princeton, N.J.: Princeton, 1959.

> This, like the Child collection, is another classic in its field. Bronson has collected the tunes to the words of the English-language ballads. For some ballads he could find no melody; for others he found several different ones. In addition to gathering the many tunes, Bronson comments on dates, origins, changes, variant types, and other topics associated with the ballads. This is truly a monumental work of perception and scholarship.

Fowler, David. **A Literary History of the Popular Ballad**. Durham,
N.C.: Duke, 1968.

This is a scholarly survey and an in-depth analysis of the English
and Scottish popular ballads from their beginnings in the fifteenth
century. Fowler explores his material to the end of the eighteenth
century. He records the influences, changes, and developments
that have taken place through the years. His work is detailed and
offers perceptive commentaries about early collected work, such
as the Percy manuscript. Beginning researchers are advised to
read the introduction in Sargent and Kittredge (described below)
before moving on to this specialized volume.

Kinsley, James, ed. **The Oxford Book of Ballads**. Oxford: Clarendon
Press, 1969.

This is a handy and easily accessible anthology of the traditional
English and Scottish ballads that does not encumber the reader
with excessive variants and scholarly apparatus yet is authentic
and well researched. It contains notes on sources, explains the
meaning of difficult terms, and offers essential historical
information. Most of the ballads are taken from the Child
collection, but some additional ones have been included.

Sargent, Helen Child, and George L. Kittredge, eds. **English and
Scottish Popular Ballads**. Boston: Houghton Mifflin, 1904.

This is a selection from the materials collected and edited by Child
and published in his compilation. Sargent and Kittredge include
all but five of the Child ballads but give only brief notes and
prefaces. There is a particularly useful introduction dealing with
the origins and characteristics of the folk ballad.

14. *Modern Bibliographical and Critical Series*

One of the most popular scholarly developments in recent years has been the publication of several continuing series of books, some devoted to authorial bibliographies and checklists, others designed to analyze various writers and literary works. Six of these series of books merit special mention because of their importance and because they furnish significant, up-to-date information needed to understand and evaluate various writers and their literary works.

Series books of this type are not published on any set schedule.

An Annotated Secondary Bibliography Series on English Literature in Transition, 1880-1920. DeKalb, Ill.: Northern Illinois University Press, 1970-

> Under the general editorship of Helmut E. Gerber, this series will issue annotated bibliographies of critical and descriptive works about Maugham, Conrad, Hardy, Forster, Galsworthy, and others. Checklists for Maugham, Conrad, Hardy, and Gissing have already appeared and are particularly worthwhile because of their accuracy and thoroughness.

The Serif Series: Bibliographies and Checklists. Kent State, Ohio: Kent State University, 1967-

> William White serves as general editor of this series, which began with a bibliography of material by and about Wilfred Owen, and has so far included some indispensable volumes, e.g., well-

annotated checklists of Malamud and Updike. These books include
a listing of the complete writings of the author in addition to a
checklist of critical studies and book reviews. The annotations are
brief but effective in conveying the principal points made by each
entry. Another significant contribution in the series is the J. R. R.
Tolkien criticism volume. Most of the books in The Serif series are
about twentieth-century authors.

Twayne's English Authors Series. New York: Twayne, 1964-

Sylvia Bowman is general editor of this ongoing series, TEAS,
which now numbers well over one hundred titles. Each book,
written by a college teacher or researcher in the subject area, gives
an outline chronology of the principal biographical facts and then
surveys the author's career. Usually stressed are influences on the
author's work, his philosophy and themes, and literary theories;
analyses of principal writings, interspersed with critical
comments, are also given. Each book contains notes and references
and a bibliography of primary and secondary sources. These
bibliographies are usually annotated in whole or in part. Although
the quality of the books varies, depending on the industry and
conscientiousness of the researcher, the volumes are useful
biographical-critical introductions. In many cases they are the
definitive studies of particular authors. While other books have
been written about the most famous authors, the Twayne series is
especially valuable because it devotes volumes to minor authors
and critics who have only been slightly discussed in literary
histories and never before been treated in such detail.

Several of the books make available for the first time primary
data, facts, bibliography, manuscript quotations, etc., in both the
chapters and the notes and reference sections. In some of the books
the footnotes themselves contain definitive information. TEAS is
a most useful and immensely serviceable series.

Twayne's United States Authors Series. New York: Twayne, 1961-

Also under the editorship of Sylvia Bowman, this series is
arranged in the same format as Twayne's English Authors Series.
Some of the volumes are unduly sketchy; others are actually
definitive pieces of work on their subject and contain a
considerable amount of original research. In addition to covering
major writers, such as Hemingway, Faulkner, Hawthorne, and
Cooper, the Twayne United States series devotes volumes to
writers who had been given too little attention and who deserve
full-length analysis—to mention a few: Dion Boucicault, Van

Wyck Brooks, Sarah Orne Jewett, George Washington Cable, Hilda Doolittle (H.D.), Harold Frederic, Maxwell Bodenheim, James Lane Allen, and Bernard DeVoto. Many readers will find most of the TUSAS studies extremely rewarding.

Twentieth Century Interpretations. Englewood Cliffs, N.J.: Prentice-Hall, 1968-

Under the general editorship of Maynard Mack, over seventy-five titles have already appeared in this continuing series. Each volume contains thoughtful, scholarly essays and analyses about famous literary works. The articles, by eminent authors, critics, and other experts, are usually the best that could be chosen. Each volume has a selected bibliography. Among the many works analyzed are Boswell's **Life of Johnson, Endgame, The Great Gatsby, Hamlet, Lord Jim, Portrait of the Artist as a Young Man, The Rape of the Lock, The Sound and the Fury, The Waste Land,** and several of Shakespeare's plays.

Twentieth Century Views. Englewood Cliffs, N.J.: Prentice-Hall, 1962-

Also edited by Maynard Mack, each volume in this continuing series offers a collection of critical essays about writers with an accompanying selected bibliography. In general, the essays are stimulating, well-researched, and valuable contributions. Among the writers analyzed are O'Neill, Miller, Swift, Twain, Hemingway, Frost, Dickens, Camus, Auden, Milton, Keats, Thomas, and Whitman. There are also books on particular topics, such as **Restoration Dramatists** and **The Modern American Theater**.

15. *Pamphlet Biographical-Critical Series*

Four series of pamphlets of critical studies are particularly useful. Each series covers a specific area of literature and is basically constructed on the same principle. The pamphlets (each averaging between forty and fifty pages) give essential biographical data about an author, offer an analysis and evaluation of that author's most important works, and conclude with a selected bibliography of the works and of secondary materials written about him or her. While some of the pamphlets are not as perceptive as others, the majority in all of the series are worthwhile introductions and guides to further investigation. Series pamphlets of this type are not necessarily published on any set schedule.

Columbia Essays on Modern Writers. New York: Columbia, 1964-

This series is especially informative in presenting studies not only of British writers of relatively recent vintage, such as Harold Pinter, but also in analyzing and surveying the work of such non-English figures as Apollinaire and de Unamuno. No American writers are included, as this series complements the Minnesota one that deals with American writers exclusively. (See below.)

Contemporary Writers in Christian Perspective. Grand Rapids, Mich.: Eerdmans, 1966-

These pamphlets are essentially focused on literary criticism. The word Christian is used in its broadest sense to include spiritual values and concepts relating to morality. Among the writers studied so far are Golding, Bellow, C. S. Lewis, Ionesco, Albee, Malamud, Updike, Salinger, Steinbeck, and Marianne Moore.

University of Minnesota Pamphlets on American Writers. Minneapolis: The University of Minnesota Press, 1959-1972.

This compilation was conceived to be the American counterpart of the British Council pamphlets (described below) and it maintained generally high standards. It treated early writers, such as Franklin and Cooper, and also evaluated the books of more recent figures, such as Wright, Welty, Mailer, and Updike. One hundred and three pamphlets were published in this series.

Most of these essays (ninety-seven of them) have been collected and published as **American Writers, A Collection of Literary Biographies**, edited by Leonard Unger (New York: Scribner, 1974). For this collection there was some updating of the material, although, in general, the changes are modest. Several of the bibliographies have, however, been made more current.

Writers and Their Work. London: Longmans, 1950-

Sponsored by the British Council, these pamphlets deal with British writers from the earliest times to the twentieth century. The accounts are well written and generally well researched. The series has an additional value in that it devotes booklets to writers, such as G. M. Trevelyan, Herbert Read, Bertrand Russell, and others, who are sometimes overlooked in the study of English literature.

16. Dictionaries and Language Guides

The correct use of words and language is an abiding concern for many of us. Although collegiate dictionaries and college handbooks are readily available and useful, there are some special and more detailed works with which all serious readers should be acquainted. The well-known **Oxford** dictionary is the most comprehensive of all, and is therefore listed first. Three standard dictionaries are listed next, and are followed by two slang dictionaries—English and American.

DICTIONARIES

Oxford English Dictionary—New English Dictionary on Historical Principles. Oxford: Clarendon Press, 1888-1933.

Often referred to as either the **OED** or the **NED**, this thirteen-volume (including supplement) classic lists almost a half-million words and gives their origin, history, and meaning. The meanings are illustrated by countless quotations from English authors. The **OED** is especially arranged to stress the historical meanings of words, including as it does various changes in denotation and connotation.

The **OED** is indispensable for historical definitions; but for readers who do not need such information, a one-volume unabridged dictionary is easier to consult for spelling, pronunciation, syllabication, and usage.

A Supplement to the Oxford English Dictionary, Volume 1 (A-C), has been published by Clarendon Press (1972). This is the first part of a freshening and updating project. In addition to word meanings, there are thousands of illustrative quotations that are arranged historically with, of course, many quotations from twentieth-century writers to indicate word use. R. W. Burchfield has edited this volume.

Clarendon has also recently published a **Compact Edition of the Oxford English Dictionary** (1971). The complete text of the **OED** has been reduced micrographically from thirteen to two volumes. A magnifying glass is included with this edition.

Funk and Wagnalls New Standard Dictionary of the English Language. New York: Funk & Wagnalls, 1913-

This is a sound, well-organized, unabridged dictionary that includes approximately half a million words. Originally issued in 1913, this dictionary is updated periodically by new editions that incorporate the latest words and record usage changes.

Random House Dictionary of the English Language, The Unabridged Edition. New York: Random House, 1966.

While it contains fewer (over 260,000) words than the other two unabridged dictionaries mentioned, this work contains definitions of many recent words, several of which are yet to be found in other dictionaries. It is also especially useful because it incorporates concise bilingual dictionaries of French, German, Spanish, and Italian.

Webster's Third New International Dictionary of the English Language, Unabridged. Springfield, Mass.: Merriam, 1961.

Containing more than 450,000 words, **Webster's New International** is probably the most frequently consulted unabridged dictionary. It has aroused much controversy because it is most liberal and permissive in listing words as standard, or at least acceptable, English: it does not use the label "colloquial," nor does it classify or comment about many words previously considered slang.

For a guide to what was once—or is still—considered slang usage or overly colloquial by some language experts and teachers, one may consult **Webster's New International Dictionary**, 2d ed. (1934), which contains over 600,000 entries, many of which are now obsolete. This edition also has such helpful features as a pronouncing gazetteer and a pronouncing biographical section—units not found in the 1961 volume. Readers would do well to consider two disparate viewpoints by language experts, one favoring the 1934 edition, the other preferring the 1961 edition. See, for example, Wilson Follett, "Sabotage in Springfield," **Atlantic Monthly** (January 1962) and Bergen Evans, "But What's a Dictionary For?" **Atlantic Monthly** (May 1962).

Partridge, Eric., ed. A Dictionary of Slang and Unconventional English. 6th ed. New York: Macmillan, 1967.

Partridge's work is a famous compilation of slang words and expressions—mostly British. In addition to giving meanings, this linguistic tool gives the source of the word and, when possible, indicates the period when the slang was used and notes whether it has become obsolete. It must be remembered, however, that Partridge records mostly British slang.

Wentworth, Harold, and Stuart Berg Flexner, eds. **Dictionary of American Slang**. New York: Thomas Y. Crowell, 1967.

This is the slang dictionary most helpful to Americans since it deals with American words and phrases. It gives the meaning of the slang expression and in many cases the origin as well. Some of the words and phrases defined are "cliffdweller," "flake out," "mensch," "dragster," "wet behind the ears," "hoosegow," "French leave," and "the nineteenth hole."

LANGUAGE GUIDES

Follett, Wilson, Jacques Barzun, and others. **Modern American Usage: A Guide**. New York: Hill and Wang, Inc., 1966.

This volume is a most helpful guide to correct American practices in grammar, style, spelling, punctuation, etc. A particularly informative section deals with idioms and jargon. Readers will find this work invaluable and should consult it when they encounter problems of language use.

Fowler, Henry W.,ed. **A Dictionary of Modern English Usage**. 2d ed., rev. by Ernest Gowers. Oxford: Clarendon Press, 1965.

This is a revision of Fowler's famous **Dictionary of Modern English Usage** (Oxford: Clarendon Press, 1926). It deals with grammar, syntax, idioms, punctuation, spelling, pronunciation, and related matters. Two qualifications must be recorded: first, Fowler's guide tends to be strict and traditional in language use and is considered too rigid and conservative for the tastes of most present-day teachers and writers; second, Fowler's primary emphasis is on British usage.

17. Style Manuals

When researchers are preparing written assignments, they must follow certain style rules, or procedures, concerning format, mechanics, and footnoting, as well as use a logical arrangement of materials. The most comprehensive style guide is the University of Chicago **Manual of Style**, which is intended for "authors, editors, and copywriters." The most commonly accepted guides for term papers and other such written assignments are Kate Turabian's **Manual** and the **MLA Style Sheet**. Many colleges and universities recommend particular handbooks for style and library research preparation; the **Harbrace College Handbook** and the **Macmillan Handbook of English** are among the most popular and reliable, and several other publishers issue similar guides. (There are also books that are somewhat similar to the traditional handbooks but are more limited in scope; perhaps the most famous of these is **The Elements of Style**, 2d ed., by William Strunk, Jr., and E. B. White [New York: Macmillan, 1972]. Strunk and White give basic rules for composition and usage, caution about misusing words and expressions, and teach an approach to correct style.) If no specific handbook or manual is recommended, a student would be well advised to follow the Turabian **Manual**, the **Student's Guide**, or the **MLA Style Sheet**.

A Manual of Style. 12th ed., rev. Chicago: The University of Chicago Press, 1969.

> This book discusses punctuation, styling techniques, footnotes, and bibliographies, etc., but is particularly geared to book preparation. There are sections on copy editing, proofreading, and design and typography. The Chicago **Manual** is very thorough in dealing with punctuation, spelling, and the handling of place names, scientific terminology, etc. Although this is a seminal book it should be consulted by the average student only to check on especially difficult stylistic matters.

MLA Style Sheet. 2d ed. New York: Modern Language Association, 1970.

This is the most popular manual of style for theses, dissertations, and articles contributed to scholarly journals. The booklet contains sections on footnoting, paper preparations, and bibliographies, with additional concise comments on mechanics, proofreading, etc. While some colleges and universities recommend the **MLA Style Sheet** for preparing term papers, it is not as complete for this purpose as are the Turabian books. For instance, not all possibilities of footnote and bibliographical examples are found in the **MLA Style Sheet**, and readers may feel that they need more particular information on preparing and documenting a paper.

Skillin, Marjorie E., Robert M. Gay, and others. **Words into Type: A Guide in the Preparation of Manuscripts; for Writers, Editors, Proofreaders and Printers**. Rev. ed. New York: Appleton-Century-Crofts, 1964.

This is an authoritative work which is commonly used by book publishers. Other readers should consult it as an ultimate reference in particularly puzzling questions, but for research paper writing, the Turabian books and the **MLA Style Sheet** should be of primary use.

Turabian, Kate L. **A Manual for Writers of Term Papers, Theses, and Dissertations**. 3d ed., rev. Chicago: The University of Chicago Press, 1967.

This handbook, based on the style recommended in the Chicago **Manual of Style**, deals with the preparation of formal papers and reports as well as more advanced dissertations. It is highly recommended for solving problems dealing with footnotes, quotations, cross-references, bibliographies, etc. Students will find this an extremely helpful guide.

Turabian, Kate L. **Student's Guide for Writing College Papers**. 2d ed., rev. Chicago: The University of Chicago Press, 1969.

This is perhaps the most useful reference devoted solely to helping undergraduates prepare a research paper. It is clear, much more basic and thorough than similar works, and definitely directed to college students. Turabian discusses choosing and narrowing a topic, collecting material, using the library, outlining, footnoting, and preparing footnotes and bibliography. She gives examples of almost every possible type of footnote and bibliographical entry. Since the book is intended specifically for undergraduate research paper preparation, it avoids scholarly technicalities that often lead to more confusion than enlightenment.

18. Literary Handbooks

Many literary handbooks give brief encyclopedia-type information about literary terms, movements, works, allusions, etc. Although there are a number of such books available, the following are especially helpful.

Abrams, M. H., ed. **A Glossary of Literary Terms.** 3d ed. New York: Holt, 1971.

> This guide is relatively brief but most helpful, with clear, concise explanations of such topics as black humor, Chicago School, objective correlative, sprung rhythm, and affective fallacy.

Gayle, Dorothy, ed. **Oxford Companion to English Literature.** 4th ed., rev. Oxford: Oxford University Press, 1967. (Previous editions were edited by Paul Harvey.)

> This voluminous reference guide contains brief articles about authors and literary works, explains common terms, allusions, and genres, and identifies many characters in drama and fiction. The latest edition adds a considerable amount of information about twentieth-century literary materials. Like the Hart volume on American literature (described next), this is an invaluable directory.

Hart, James D., ed. **Oxford Companion to American Literature.** 4th ed. New York: Oxford University Press, 1965.

> This is the most used one-volume compendium of data about American literature. It gives brief biographies of authors, summarizes significant stories and novels, discusses literary schools and movements, and explains various references and terms.

Harvey, Paul, ed. **Oxford Companion to Classical Literature.** Oxford: Clarendon Press, 1940.

> This collection is extremely useful in furnishing information about basic Greek and Latin materials—authors, literary works, and terms—which aid in a full understanding of English literature.

Harvey, Paul, and Janet E. Heseltine, eds. **Oxford Companion to French Literature**. Oxford: Clarendon Press, 1959.

> Since so much interaction has taken place between English and French literature from the time of the Norman Conquest to the present, it is valuable to have this reliable reference listing French writers, literary movements, concepts, and terms.

Holman, C. Hugh, ed. **A Handbook to Literature**. 3d ed. New York: Odyssey, 1972.

> This latest edition of the **Handbook** is based on the original volume of the same title by William F. Thrall and Addison Hibbard, which has been used by thousands of students since it was first published in 1936. The book was first revised and enlarged by C. Hugh Holman in 1960, and the third edition has added further entries. This guide covers a wide range of subjects and terms. Among the items identified are dithyramb, Hebraism, Grub Street, pleonasm, Spenserian stanza, poet laureate, and humanism. This handbook also adds an outline of principal literary events in the history of English and American literature. The latest edition lists Nobel and Pulitzer Prize winners as well as National Book Award winners.

Preminger, Alex, and others, eds. **Encyclopedia of Poetry**. New enl. ed. Princeton, N.J.: Princeton, 1975.

> This is a valuable, immensely useful compendium that explains various concepts, and types, of poetry and presents commentary about the history, theories, and techniques of verse from its origins to the present day. This very scholarly volume discusses poetry from all parts of the world.

Shaw, Harry. **Dictionary of Literary Terms**. New York: McGraw-Hill, 1972.

> A particularly useful guide because of its up-to-date material and numerous excellent examples, Shaw's work also includes many references to journalism, films, the theater, and television.

Shipley, Joseph T. **Dictionary of World Literature**. Rev. ed. New York: Philosophical Library, 1953.

> This basic reference work concentrates on literary criticism and various literary schools and movements associated with the major languages. It has brief but helpful surveys of English, French, German, and Russian criticism and includes a considerable number of literary terms and elements. Shipley's **Dictionary** has been compiled with the help of an impressive number of advisers and contributors.

19. *Basic Scholarly Journals*

Perhaps no other field of study contains as voluminous a number of periodicals and journals devoted to one subject as does that of literature. Any listing of such publications must therefore be highly selective, as there are so many journals—e.g., **Essays in Criticism, Papers on Language and Literature, Studies in the Novel, Texas Studies in Language and Literature**, to mention just a few—that deserve comment. Accordingly, only those journals that students would probably consult most frequently have been chosen for the following list. Bibliographies in many of the journals will lead to additional periodicals to which one may refer.

Abstracts of English Studies, 1958-   [Monthly, Sept.-June]

> Now published ten times a year, this periodical (with editorial offices at the University of Colorado) takes a selected number of magazines and presents an annotated bibliography of the articles appearing in them. The abstracts attempt to present the essential contents as objectively as possible. This is an indispensable guide for keeping abreast of current materials, but since it is selective in its choice of journals it obviously does not present a comprehensive bibliography.

American Literature, 1929-   [Quarterly]

> This quarterly, published by Duke University Press, is the most prestigious journal in its subject area. In recent years, more articles have been published on twentieth-century literature than ever before. The pages of this journal are devoted to scholarly articles and notes distinguished by depth of research and fresh insights. **AL** also reviews books and publishes in each issue a bibliography of articles on American literature appearing in current periodicals. **AL** has a research-in-progress as well as a queries section.

American Quarterly, 1949-   [Irregularly; see below]

> Sponsored by the American Studies Association and the University of Pennsylvania, **AQ** is published five times a year and presents articles on American subjects in all periods. Although

only some of its essays deal with literature, its wide scope allows for treatment of other materials which are often of interest to those in the field of English. It contains articles on art and architecture, economics, education, folklore, history, language, philosophy, psychology, religion, sociology, etc. Such interdisciplinary studies frequently touch literary topics. AQ issues an annual selective bibliography dealing with all subjects related to American culture and civilization. (This bibliography is very briefly annotated.) It also furnishes a yearly list of interdisciplinary dissertations completed and in progress.

American Speech: A Quarterly of Linguistic Usage, 1925/6- [Quarterly]

This journal, sponsored by Columbia University Press, publishes articles and notes relating to language use and study. It is an indispensable source of information on pronunciations, dialects, changes in word meaning, place and family names, and allied subjects. Typical titles are "Washington Irving and Frontier Speech," "Etymology, Anglo-Saxon, and Noah Webster," and "Imperative and Subjunctive in Contemporary English." It contains interesting studies of the origins and development of meanings, such as "aerospace," "gremlin," and "gung ho."

Bulletin of Bibliography, 1897-   [Quarterly]

Published by the library reference materials firm of F. W. Faxon Company, this journal is famous for its immensely useful checklists and bibliographies. Among the countless number of writers who have been studied bibliographically are Baldwin, McCullers, Capote, Purdy, Wright, Priestley, Singer, Cary, Agee, and MacNeice. In addition to author checklists of primary and secondary materials, **BB** also issues up-to-date addenda to checklists previously published in books and in other sources. Further, its scope allows it to contain bibliographies of some earlier writers, for instance, Sir Thomas Wyatt and John Lydgate, as well as checklist articles with titles like "The Influence of the Bible on American Literature: A Review of Research from 1955 to 1965," "Synge Criticism, 1907-1967," and "The Hollywood Novel: A Partial Bibliography." **BB** is an indispensable work for researchers, especially for those interested in contemporary literature.

Bulletin of the New York Public Library, 1897-   [Quarterly]

Originally a monthly (except for July and August), until the end of

1971, this journal became a quarterly and now publishes scholarly research articles pertaining to materials in the special collections of the New York Public Library as well as essays dealing with more general matters and with manuscripts located in other places. To give a sampling of subjects: there have been articles on the diaries of Virginia Woolf, on Boswell, on Blake's **Tiriel,** on the reception of Synge's **Playboy of the Western World** in Ireland and America, and on the revisions in Hardy's **The Woodlanders.** It also issues checklists of criticism about many authors, e.g., Clough, Bowen, Jarrell, Arthur Miller, etc. It contains articles and materials on other subjects, areas, but the emphasis is on literary topics. Publication was temporarily discontinued with the December 1971 issue (volume 75), because of budgetary problems, but it was resumed and a large volume was published for 1972.

College English, 1939-   [Monthly, Oct.-May]

This journal is published by the National Council of Teachers of English. Since it deals with teaching problems, techniques, issues, and developments, it is intended primarily for English faculties. There are, however, many articles of interest to nonteaching audiences, although most of the essays were published before the 1960s. Articles such as "The Bible and **The Grapes of Wrath,**" "Illusion and Reality in the Medieval Drama," and "**The Glass Menagerie:** Three Visions of Time," are typical of the general-interest essays. In recent years the journal has become more narrow, leaning toward linguistics, morphology, and intimate studies of language.

Comparative Literature, 1948-   [Quarterly]

Published by the University of Oregon, this journal emphasizes the interrelation between literary works and authors of various countries and discusses the similarities between, and relationships among, different writers. The masthead page notes that this journal is interested in "the theory of literature, movements, genres, periods, and authors—from the earliest times to the present." Typical articles are "Yeats and Goethe," "Lady Philosophy in Boethius and Dante," "T. S. Eliot and the Austere Poetics of Valéry," and "Turgenev's Aesthetic and Western Realism."

Critique: Studies in Modern Fiction, 1956/57-   [Triannually]

Issued from its editorial office at the Georgia Institute of Technology, **Critique** presents particularly informative essays on present-day authors of fiction, especially the more fashionable figures such as Beckett, Hawkes, Vonnegut, Jr., and Kesey. It also treats lesser-known writers and up-and-coming talent, and studies modern novels like **Catch-22**. It occasionally publishes bibliographies on individual authors and devotes articles to fiction in other areas, such as Africa and Asia.

ELH, 1934-   [Quarterly]

Originally called **ELH: A Journal of English Literary History**, this periodical now uses just the initials. Issued from Johns Hopkins University Press, it publishes stimulating scholarly articles covering all periods of English and American literature, but the bulk of its essays center on British authors from the Renaissance to the end of the nineteenth century. It published an annual bibliography on the Romantic movement during the years 1936-1949.

English Language Notes, 1963/4-   [Quarterly]

Issued from the University of Colorado, this journal publishes short, well-researched articles and notes pertaining to English and American language and literature. Typical titles are "More Manuscript Versions of Poems by Sidney," "The Musical Meaning of 'Mode' in **2 Henry IV**," "The Probable Identity of Hopkins' 'Two Beautiful Young People,'" and "Hart Crane's 'Voyages VI,' Stanza 6." The explications of lines, passages, allusions, etc., are generally first-rate. It publishes annually a selective bibliography of the Romantic movement as a supplement to its September issue. Many of the bibliographic items are annotated with descriptive or critical comments, and sometimes brief summaries of contents are given. This bibliography began in the September 1965 issue and covered the research done in the previous year.

English Literature in Transition, 1880-1920, 1957-   [Quarterly]

For many years **ELT** was issued from Northern Illinois University. It is now published from the English department at Arizona State. Helmut Gerber has continued as editor. **ELT** contains articles, bibliographies, and notes on English authors writing during the years mentioned in the title. Among the authors emphasized are Conrad, Wells, Galsworthy, Hardy, Kipling, Lawrence, Forster, Ford, Wilde, Owen, etc. Up-to-date current bibliographies (many annotated), news, and notes on writers in this period are also published.

Explicator, 1942-   [Monthly, Sept.-June]

This bulletin, now issued by Virginia Commonwealth University in Richmond, provides a clearinghouse for textual analysis. Short essays or notes interpret the meaning of certain poems or lines and analyze allusions, characters, and passages in American and English stories and novels. This periodical provides a useful forum for eliminating textual obscurities by furnishing intensive analyses. Its yearly index is most useful.

Journal of English and Germanic Philology, 1897-   [Quarterly]

This publication, emanating from the University of Illinois, deals with English, German, and Scandinavian languages and literature. The articles are erudite and cover a wide range of material. The title is rather misleading because most of the articles are scholarly essays on works of literature and are not limited to very specialized linguistic areas.

MLA. See **PMLA**.

Modern Drama, 1958-   [Quarterly]

This periodical, originally issued from the Department of English, University of Kansas, and sponsored by A. C. Edwards, has, beginning with the December 1972 issue (volume 15, number 3), been published by the Graduate Center for Study of Drama at the University of Toronto. **Modern Drama** analyzes drama and dramatists since Ibsen. Its articles and book reviews dealing with the theater in all countries are generally stimulating and scholarly. From September 1960 to September 1968, **Modern Drama** published a selective bibliography of books and articles dealing with contemporary drama, conveniently arranged by country and author. One special number a year is devoted to a particular writer or subject, such as "German Drama Since World War II." **An Analytical Index to Modern Drama, Vols. I XIII** was published in 1973 by the Hakkert Press of Toronto.

Modern Fiction Studies, 1955-   [Quarterly]

MFS, sponsored by the Department of English of Purdue University, devotes two issues—its Spring and Autumn numbers—to an individual writer, a school of writers, or a particular topic Thus, there have been issues on such authors as James, Greene, Dostoevsky, Stephen Crane, Hardy, American realists, etc. Each issue dealing with an individual writer has a selected bibliography about that writer. The other two yearly issues (the general numbers) contain articles and book reviews about modern novelists (that is, novelists of roughly the past hundred years). The book review section is the only weak unit in this journal. One reviewer generally reviews several books in the same essay. As a result, individual reviews tend to be sketchy and oversimplified, and sometimes the commentaries lack balance and objectivity.

Modern Language Quarterly, 1940-   [Quarterly]

The University of Washington at Seattle sponsors this journal, which contains scholarly articles and book reviews dealing with all periods of literature. Some sample articles are "The Radical Irony of **Hedda Gabler**," "The Voices of Marvell's Lyrics," and "The Problem of Symbolist Form in Melville's 'Bartleby the Scrivener.' " Up to 1963 it published an annual bibliography of Arthurian studies.

Modern Language Review, 1905-   [Quarterly]

Issued by the Modern Humanities Research Association from the University of Birmingham, England, this scholarly journal publishes original articles on language and literature as well as hitherto unpublished texts and documents. **MLR** deals mainly with British and Continental literature. Most of the articles concern topics from the Medieval period to the Victorian era. It publishes very little about American writers.

Modern Philology, 1903-   [Quarterly]

Issued from the University of Chicago, this scholarly journal stresses articles (although it sometimes publishes shorter notes) covering all fields of literature from the Old English period to the present. Typical titles are "Grendel: A New Aspect," "The Ideas of Byzantium in William Morris and W. B. Yeats," and "Medieval English Literature and the Question of Unity." **MP** also issues book reviews and lengthy review articles. From 1932 to 1957 it published an exceedingly important bibliography of studies in Victorian literature, which was then picked up by **Victorian Studies** (see below).

Nineteenth-Century Fiction, 1945-   [Quarterly]

Issued by the University of California Press, this journal is comprised of articles, notes, and reviews of books dealing with the

Victorian novel and short stories. Although it does discuss some American writers, most of the materials relate to British novelists. Without question, this is a highly essential publication. From 1945 to 1949 it was more limited in scope and was called **The Trollopian: A Journal Devoted to Studies in Anthony Trollope and His Contemporaries in Victorian Fiction.**

Notes and Queries, 1849/50- [Monthly]

Oxford University Press sponsors this journal, which publishes brief articles and short notes of all types—bibliographical, textual, biographical—and on all kinds of subjects—literary influences, sources, etc. Typical subject titles are "Two Unpublished Wordsworth Letters," "Some Hazlitt Quotations and Their Sources," and "Rare and Unrecorded Publications of Smollett's Works." **Notes and Queries** is especially helpful in publishing readers' questions about various literary issues and problems, e.g., sources of quotations, location of letters and manuscripts, and particular editions (the 1749 edition of "The Vanity of Human Wishes" containing an additional couplet in the autograph of Samuel Johnson, for instance). Answers are supplied by various scholars, librarians, and researchers. This bulletin also reviews books.

Papers of the Bibliographical Society of America, 1906- [Quarterly]

This is a very scholarly journal (with editorial offices in the University of Texas [Austin] English Department) that publishes articles, bibliographical notes, and book reviews. Covering all periods of literature, **PBSA** issues valuable information on editions of books, textual variants, authorial drafts, and similar data. These are the types of articles found in this publication: "Smollett's Revisions of **Roderick Random,**" "**Of Time and the River:** The Final Editing," and "The Manuscript and the Text of James Agee's **A Death in the Family.**" **PBSA** occasionally publishes worthwhile checklists of individual writers.

Philological Quarterly, 1922- [Quarterly]

Issued by the State University of Iowa, **PQ** covers all periods of writing from ancient classical to contemporary and deals with both language study and literature. It contains scholarly notes as well as longer research studies. In general, it does not print many articles on twentieth-century literature, and reviews only a few books. **PQ** publishes its invaluable current bibliography of English literature 1660-1800 in its July issue.

PMLA. Publications of the Modern Language Association of America, 1885-   [Quarterly]

This prestigious scholarly journal is published quarterly, with supplementary issues containing programs of meetings and a directory listing the members of the Modern Language Association. **PMLA** publishes scholarly, carefully researched articles on all periods of literature of various countries, with the bulk of the articles written on English and American literature. Its annual bibliography started modestly in 1922 to cover material published in 1921 and has developed into a superlative compilation called the **MLA International Bibliography**, now published separately.

Review of English Studies: A Quarterly Journal of English Literature and the English Language, 1925-   [Quarterly]

This publication, published by Oxford University Press, prints articles, notes, and book reviews. It presents a consistently well-researched and valuable group of materials, and the book review section is one of the best in any scholarly journal. **RES** covers all periods of British literature, although not many essays concern twentieth-century writers.

Speculum, 1926-   [Quarterly]

Issued from Cambridge, Massachusetts, and published by the Mediaeval Academy of America, this is an immensely erudite journal devoted to medieval studies. It contains book reviews as well as articles; the review section is especially extensive and the judgments expressed are knowledgeable and sensible. In addition to dealing with major topics such as **Beowulf**, Chaucer, and Malory, **Speculum** has in-depth information about satellite figures and currents that give considerable depth and comprehensiveness to the subject material.

Studies in Bibliography, 1948/9-   [Annually]

Published by the Bibliographical Society of the University of Virginia, **SB** issues scholarly articles on all areas of literature with emphasis on bibliographical and textual subjects. Some typical subjects are "Two 'New Texts' of Thomas Hardy's **The**

Woodlanders," "Richardson's Revisions of **Pamela**," and "Light on Joyce's **Exiles?** A New Manuscript, a Curious Analogue, and Some Speculations." **SB** issues an annual selected checklist of bibliographical scholarship for the previous year.

Studies in Philology, 1906-   [Quarterly]

Issued by the Department of English at the University of North Carolina, **SP** publishes well-researched and meaningful scholarly articles covering many periods and a wide variety of materials, but emphasis is on the Medieval and Renaissance periods. Typical articles are "Neo-Latin Biblical Pastoral," "Thomas More's Use of Humor," and "A Re-Evaluation of Hellenism in the French Renaissance." Until 1921 it listed books concerned with the Renaissance; then, with volume 19, in 1922, it commenced an annual bibliography on the literature of the Renaissance which continued until the May 1969 issue. **SP** now devotes one of its yearly numbers to studies in the Renaissance.

Studies in Short Fiction, 1963-   [Quarterly]

This journal from Newberry College, Newberry, South Carolina, is devoted to articles and notes analyzing short works of fiction. While some consideration is given to European literature, the journal deals mostly with textual analysis of English and American literary works. Although the quality and value of the material is uneven, many well-researched and provocative articles appear. Only a small number of books are reviewed. Published in each summer issue is an annual bibliography of analyses of significant short fiction. Of necessity selective, this checklist is nonetheless useful.

Twentieth Century Literature, 1955-   [Quarterly]

Originally published by Alan Swallow in Denver, **TCL** was later issued from Immaculate Heart College in Los Angeles and, since 1974, has been published at Hofstra University. **TCL** is a scholarly critical journal devoted mainly to analyzing the works of important contemporary authors and furnishing current bibliography. Each issue contains a selected bibliography of articles about twentieth-century authors and selected special subjects, such as the theater of the absurd, comparative literature, and literary theory. The current bibliographical items are annotated in order to give the gist of each article in one or two sentences. In addition, this journal publishes helpful separate checklists on individual writers and in various subject areas, e.g., Auden, Pinter, and African writing in English.

Victorian Studies, 1957-   [Quarterly]

This journal, sponsored by Indiana University, deals not just with literature but also with art, social problems, history, and other aspects of the Victorian period. The majority of the articles, however, deal with English literary figures and works and show an excellent awareness of the latest scholarship of this era. The journal also publishes annually a Victorian bibliography which should be required reading for all those involved with Victorian literature.

20. Creative-Critical Journals

Several journals devote attention not only to scholarly critical articles but also to creative work—primarily poems and short stories. Some of them intersperse essays on literary topics with others on history, current events, philosophy, etc. Most of us are already acquainted with the more popular and widely circulated of these periodicals, such as **The Atlantic** and **Harper's**, but the specialist in the humanities should become familar with several other journals which have valued reputations. Again, the following list must perforce be highly selective. All entries are quarterlies.

Hudson Review, 1948—

> This journal, with editorial offices in New York City, publishes intelligent and informative articles on various subjects, has stimulating stories and verse, and contains a respected book review section. There are many articles about literature, with particular emphasis on the twentieth century. Sample titles include "The Achievement of William Empson," "Pinter's **Homecoming**: The Shock of Nonrecognition," and "Stevens: The Realistic Oriole." Distinguished authors frequently write for the **Hudson Review**: Nabokov, Frye, Gold, Bellow, among others.

Kenyon Review, 1939-1970.

> Because of financial difficulties, this splendid journal, originating from Kenyon College in Ohio, has ceased publication, but its thirty-two volumes will be a continued treasure trove for the student of literature. It published many excellent short stories and poems and was especially notable for its early writings on the "New Criticism" and its regular articles about literary criticism. The work of Ransom, Burke, Read, Steiner, and countless other significant critics graced its pages and rendered it an indispensable periodical for the literati.

111

Partisan Review, 1934-

Now published from Rutgers University, this periodical deals primarily with social and political issues from, as the title implies, a partisan liberal point of view. It does not publish as many essays on literature as many of its readers would wish, but occasional stimulating articles appear with titles such as "The Other Lawrence," "The Jamesian Lie," and "On James Dickey." Almost all its literary articles are about twentieth-century authors.

Sewanee Review, 1892-

As the editors of this journal like to emphasize, this is America's oldest literary quarterly. Published by the University of the South, Sewanee, Tennessee, it includes stories, poems, and book reviews, and devotes all its articles to literary subjects. The materials are practically always of high quality, and it is almost impossible not to find much in every issue which will be of interest and of value to the student of literature. Sample titles are "The Narrator of **Paradise Lost**," "**Absalom, Absalom!**: The Historian as Detective," and "**Macbeth**: The Great Illusion."

South Atlantic Quarterly, 1902-

While not technically a creative journal because it does not publish poems or stories, this publication (sponsored by Duke University Press) yields many worthwhile essays on literature. Most of its literary articles are concerned with twentieth-century figures, such as Forster, Orwell, Tate, Cary, Golding, Wolfe, Burke, and Styron. It also has an excellent book review section and a top-rank group of reviewers.

Southern Review, 1965-

Published by Louisiana State University, this relatively new periodical has captured much attention in literary circles. It has covered a wide variety of subjects—Melville, Verlaine, Claudel, Yeats, Conrad, James, Winters, Swift, Hardy, to mention a few—and has published verse and stories by notable authors, such as Isaac Bashevis Singer and Joyce Carol Oates.

Virginia Quarterly Review, 1925-

VQR (sponsored by the University of Virginia) contains stories, poems, and book reviews and treats many subject areas besides literature. While not as many essays about literary subjects appear as one would wish—considering the high standards of this journal—a considerable range of material is discussed and analyzed. Some sample articles are "Shaw's Tragicomic Irony," "Emerson and Hawthorne: Trust and Doubt," and "Faulkner's **Sanctuary** and the Southern Myth."

Western Humanities Review, 1947-

Emanating from the University of Utah and originally concentrating on subjects relating to the American West, the **Review** has broadened its outlook and includes literary essays on a wide variety of topics, with articles on history, political matters, etc.; but most of the materials deal with literature. The work is occasionally uneven, but always thought-provoking. The following are examples of some articles which have appeared in recent years: "Chaucer's Failure With Women: The Inadequacy of Criseyde," "Malamud's Trial: **The Fixer** and the Critics," and "The Forsyte Saga Reconsidered: The Case of the Common Reader Versus Literary Criticism."

Yale Review, 1892-

This Yale University publication has had a long, impressive history. It deals with all subject areas and attracts eminent contributors and creative writers. Its literary essays run a considerable gamut. Articles on such topics as "Crime and Punishment in the **Odyssey**," and "Pirandello Old and New" are typical; and one even finds fascinating personal material, such as Robert Penn Warren explaining the relationship between his stay in Louisiana in the days of Huey Long and **All the King's Men**.

21. *Journals on Individual Authors*

One of the most useful sources of material for both general information and up-to-date research data is the specialized journal devoted to an individual writer. Such publications vary quite widely in the number of times they appear annually. They are produced by specialists and enthusiasts who are exceedingly knowledgeable about the subject matter and, in addition to essays, book reviews, queries, and notes, the latest bibliographical information is usually presented. Further, if one writes to the editor(s) of a specialized journal for particular information, one will in all likelihood receive a helpful and gracious reply.

Professor Margaret C. Patterson has compiled an impressive checklist of these publications: "V.I.P. Publications: An International Bibliography of 300 Newsletters, Journals, and Miscellanea," **Bulletin of Bibliography**, XXX (October-December 1973), 156-169. In addition to authors, this checklist includes statesmen, composers, and artists.

A listing of a few of these specialized journals should give an idea of some of the more significant titles and indicate their content and general approach.

The Dickensian, 1905-   [Triannually]

> This magazine is published by the Dickens Fellowship in London at 48 Doughty Street, where Charles Dickens lived from 1837 to 1839. It prints new material dealing with any aspect of Dickens's life and writings. During its history, The Dickensian has published materials by such famous authors as George Bernard Shaw, Angela Thirkell, Compton Mackenzie, etc., as well as by Dickens enthusiasts from every station in life. This periodical is really essential reading for students of Dickens, the Victorian period, and the Victorian mood. An index to the first 30 volumes (1905-1934) was published by the Dickens Fellowship in 1935.

Emily Dickinson Bulletin, 1968-   [Quarterly]

> This publication deals with the life and writing of Dickinson and

also with figures associated with her. It is sponsored by Professor Frederick L. Morey; its editorial address is 4508 38th Street, Brentwood, Maryland. It presents a useful compilation of the latest scholarship, discoveries, and interpretations and also publishes essays, notes, commentaries, critical exegeses, book reviews, and bibliographies. In addition, it issues data about the Dickinson home in Amherst, current meetings about Dickinson, and events involving Dickinsoniana.

Fitzgerald/Hemingway Annual, 1969-   [Annually]

Microcard Editions, Washington, D.C. issues this compilation of articles about Fitzgerald and Hemingway. It contains research articles of various lengths about the two writers' lives and writings. Previously unpublished letters are given and other unusual or rare materials are recorded; for example, "Dearly Beloved," a story by Fitzgerald which had hitherto not appeared in print, has attracted much attention. The editor, Matthew J. Bruccoli, now at the University of South Carolina, was also the editor of this compilation's predecessor, a **Fitzgerald Newsletter**, which was published four times a year from 1958 to 1968. In addition to its forty issues this newsletter published a special Winter 1963 number which consisted of a five-year index of the previous issues. These forty issues are a rich mine of Fitzgerald information. There are book reviews, textual studies, checklists of references and general bibliography, information about Fitzgerald letters, as well as numerous articles. Some sample titles are "Fitzgerald and the Princeton Triangle Club"; "Henry James: Fitzgerald's Literary Ancestor"; and "Fitzgerald the Lecturer." The notes deal with every conceivable aspect of Fitzgerald data; for example, even the make of car involved in the fatal accident in **The Great Gatsby** is ascertained. The issues which appeared between 1958 and 1968 are now conveniently collected in one volume and published by Microcard Editions (1969).

James Joyce Quarterly, 1963-   [Quarterly]

Sponsored by the University of Tulsa, this excellent journal issues stimulating and perceptive articles concentrating especially on Joyce's stories and novels. It also gives shorter notes which cover all phases of Joyce's career as both a man and a writer. Bibliographical materials frequently appear as do reviews of the latest book-length scholarship. **JJQ** generates interest by presenting opposing views on various Joyce problems and by discussing the meanings of Joycean allusions, references, and symbols. Some sample titles are "**Ulysses** and the 'Eighth and Ninth Book of Moses,' " "Joyce and Cryptology," and " 'Dubliners' and Vico."

Keats-Shelley Journal, 1952-   [Annually]

Published by the Keats-Shelley Association of America, Inc., this periodical also treats the work of Lord Byron, Leigh Hunt, and the other figures associated particularly with Shelley. It publishes essays, brief notes, and news, and issues a current bibliography of research done on Keats, Shelley, and related subject matter by scholars from all parts of the world. This journal is indispensable to the student of the English Romantic period.

Mark Twain Journal, 1936-   [Biannually]

Under the sponsorship of the Mark Twain Society, with editorial offices in Kirkwood, Missouri, this periodical issues all types of articles and material about Twain's biography and writing, stressing influences on his work, critical exegeses, personal reminiscences, picturesque anecdotes, etc. Typical titles are "The Picaresque as a Flow in Mark Twain's Novels," "Two Recently Discovered Letters by Mark Twain," and "Huck and Hamlet: An Examination of Twain's Use of Shakespeare." This publication was originally entitled the **Mark Twain Quarterly**. See also **The Twainian**.

Shakespeare Newsletter, 1951-   [Bimonthly]

Edited by Louis Marder, who is presently at the University of Illinois, Chicago Circle, this bulletin appears six times a year. It does not issue a current bibliography but from time to time publishes bibliographies on specific topics, for example, "Shakespeare and the Army," and "Shakespeare and Medicine." It presents information on various productions and performances, for example, Judith Anderson's **Hamlet**. It contains articles as well as reviews of some current important articles on Shakespeare. More gossipy in general and less thorough than the **Shakespeare Quarterly**, this newsletter often makes interesting reading.

Shakespeare Quarterly, 1950-   [Quarterly]

Founded by the Shakespeare Association of America in New York City, this journal deals with all aspects of Shakespeare's life, works, and times. There are valuable reviews of the latest research on Shakespeare as well as commentaries about the newest offerings of his plays at various festivals. There is also information concerning New York and London productions. The most valuable feature of this publication is the yearly annotated bibliography of Shakespeare studies. Since 1972, **SQ** has been published by The Folger Shakespeare Library, Washington, D.C.

The Shavian: The Journal of the Shaw Society, 1953-   [Triannually]

This British publication commenced its new series of issues in 1953, after having begun its life as the **Shaw Society Bulletin** (fifty issues published between 1946 and 1952). Currently this journal publishes articles, notes, and book reviews and considers Shaw's associations and influences. It also furnishes a summary of papers and speeches given at the Shaw Society meetings and presents useful information about productions of Shaw's plays.

The Shaw Review, 1951-   [Triannually]

This is another stimulating specialized journal. Published by Pennsylvania State University Press, this periodical prints articles, reviews, and news and also deals with questions concerning Shaw's life and work as well as his relationship to contemporary figures and his influence on other writers and thinkers. This review also publishes a very helpful annotated bibliography of the latest Shaw research.

Thoreau Society Bulletin, 1941-   [Quarterly]

Issued by the Thoreau Society (editorial offices at State University College, Geneseo, New York), this bulletin appeared originally only once or twice a year, but since 1944 it has been issued quarterly. It contains stimulating and informative articles, data, commentary, and interpretations about Thoreau's life, writing, philosophy, and the geographical areas where he lived and visited. Some issues have especially fine bibliographies of current Thoreau scholarship and publications. Reports on walking tours, notes, queries, data on the annual meeting of the Thoreau Society, cartoons, and almost any conceivable material relating to Thoreau appear frequently.

The Twainian, 1939-   [Bimonthly]

Published by the Mark Twain Research Foundation, Perry, Missouri, this bulletin is concerned mainly with "the wisdom of Mark Twain as taught by his life and writings." It prints a potpourri of material. Nineteenth-century commentaries on Twain are reproduced to make them generally available to modern readers. Annotations of some current Twain scholarship published in other journals are furnished. Twain's marginal notes, made in books that he owned, are printed. **The Twainian** also furnishes a forum for personal reminiscences, such as George Ade's "One Afternoon with Mark Twain." See also **Mark Twain Journal**.

22. Basic Concordances

A concordance is an index of words in a particular work. The earliest concordances were compiled to help readers locate particular passages from the Bible and from the works of Shakespeare. Concordances give the location of each significant word and usually quote the context in which each word appears. The usual arrangement is to list the words alphabetically, then to quote the line or passage in which the word appears, e.g.

surges
>   As the bleak incense surges, cloud on cloud,

Nightpiece 16

The verse line's number—in this case line 16 from the poem "Nightpiece"—is added after the poem's title so that the passage in which the word occurs can be located quickly.

Concordances enable readers to find immediately famous passages and other sections of interest; they also help readers in the study of poetic imagery, word choices, and word connotations, thus furnishing the raw material for analyzing an author's approach and techniques. Many concordances are now produced rapidly and effectively by using computers to program the words.

A few of the more popular and important concordances are mentioned below.

Baker, Arthur E., ed. **A Concordance to the Poetical and Dramatic Works of Alfred, Lord Tennyson**. New York: Macmillan, 1914. Reprint, New York: Barnes & Noble, 1966.

> This volume contains over 150,000 quotations and references and is particularly important because so many notable literary passages and quotations have their origins in Tennyson's work.

Baldwin, Dane L., and others, eds. **A Concordance to the Poems of John Keats**. Washington, D.C.: Carnegie Institution, 1917. Reprint, Gloucester, Mass.; Peter Smith Publisher, 1963.

This reference study notes the size of Keats's poetic vocabulary—much larger than one would expect—and furnishes an authoritative reference to his special mannerisms, e.g., using derivatives from the same root, using unusual adverbs, etc.

Bevan, E. Dean, comp. **A Concordance to the Plays and Prefaces of Bernard Shaw**. 10 vols. Detroit: Gale Research Company, 1972.

This work omits some Shaw play material and related writings, but it is a monumental undertaking and its value for Shaw studies cannot be overestimated.

Borrello, Alfred E., ed. **A Concordance of the Poetry in English of Gerard Manley Hopkins**. Metuchen, N.J.: Scarecrow Press, 1969.

Students of modern poetry will find this an especially useful concordance because of Hopkins's considerable influence. It records his brilliant vocabulary, effective use of compounds, vivid and frequently startling imagery, and enables one to examine the words both in sharp isolation and in their relation to the meaning of the whole poem.

Eby, Edwin H., ed. **A Concordance of Walt Whitman's** Leaves of Grass **and Selected Prose Writings**. Seattle: University of Washington Press, 1955.

This concordance indexes the vocabulary of the following prose pieces: "Democratic Vistas"; "A Backward Glance O'er Travel'd Roads"; "Preface" to the 1855 edition of **Leaves of Grass**; "Preface," 1872; "Preface," 1876; and "Preface Note to Second Annex."

Erdman, David V., ed. **A Concordance to the Writings of William Blake**. Ithaca, N.Y.: Cornell, 1967.

Erdman's preface is especially stimulating in discussing the possibilities of concordance use. He discovers, for example, that Blake used "death" very frequently and used "night" more than "day." This concordance study also shows differences as well as similarities among poets; for instance, Blake's vocabulary has little in common with Yeats's, thus demonstrating mythic, symbolic, and thematic distinctions.

Ingram, William, and Kathleen Swaim, eds. **A Concordance to Milton's English Poetry**. New York: Oxford University Press, 1972.

This volume gives a superb recording of the vocabulary of **Paradise Lost** as well as of Milton's other verse. It includes additional material from rough drafts and passages and variant readings of material both in print and in manuscript which is not found in the earlier Milton concordance by John Bradshaw (originally printed in London, by Sonnenheim, and reprinted in Connecticut, by Archon/Shoe String, 1965).

Parrish, Stephen Maxfield, ed. **A Concordance to the Poems of W. B. Yeats**. Ithaca, N.Y.: Cornell, 1963.

This work is of immense value because it helps to catalog Yeats's intensely poetic world of myth, legend, and private symbol: his symbolist imagination can be studied in complete detail.

Rosenbaum, S. P., ed. **A Concordance to the Poems of Emily Dickinson**. Ithaca, N.Y.: Cornell, 1964.

This reference work enables one to gain an accurate picture of Dickinson's work since hitherto isolated lines and stanzas which appear in the earlier editions of her poetry as separate works, because of incomplete knowledge at the time, are now placed in their proper poetic units. This concordance also includes variant word choices which throw further light on her working procedures and artistic selections.

Spevack, Marvin, ed. **The Harvard Concordance to Shakespeare**. Cambridge, Mass.: Harvard, 1973.

This study is one of the most impressive reference volumes ever published. It records every significant word used in the plays and the poems and notes whether or not the word is used in a prose or a verse context. It surpasses John Bartlett's earlier Shakespeare concordance (1894, reprint 1963) in thoroughness.

Tatlock, John S. P., and Arthur G. Kennedy, eds. **A Concordance to the Complete Works of Geoffrey Chaucer and to the Romaunt of the Rose**. Washington, D.C.: Carnegie Institution, 1927. Reprint Gloucester, Mass.: Peter Smith Publisher, 1963.

This book is an indispensable tool for studying the development of the English language and the vocabulary of Middle English, as well as for gaining a more thorough knowledge of Chaucer's vocabulary.

23. *Professional Organizations*

There are countless professional organizations in the field of literature. Some of these groups deal with specific periods; e.g., the Early English Text Society, which publishes definitive editions of works primarily from the Anglo-Saxon and Middle English periods; the Renaissance English Text Society, which issues scarce books from the 1475-1660 period; and the Augustan Reprint Society, which publishes works from the seventeenth and eighteenth centuries.

Then there are organizations devoted to individual writers; e.g., the Thoreau Society, which is intended to increase knowledge of, and interest in, the life and writings of Henry David Thoreau. This group, open to anyone interested in Thoreau, holds an annual meeting in Concord, Massachusetts. There is a Kipling Society, a James Joyce Society, an Emerson Society, two Shakespeare societies, two George Bernard Shaw groups, two Mark Twain groups, and countless others. Since almost all such organizations publish periodicals or newsletters, further information, if desired, can be obtained from **Ulrich's International Periodical Directory**, from the Gerstenberger and Hendrick **Directory**, the Meserole and Bishop list, or from the **Encyclopedia of Associations** (see Index for references).

There are, however, at least four organizations which should, in a book of this nature, be described in more detail. Basic information on these four is given below.

College English Association (CEA). Oakland University, Rochester, Mich. 48063. Executive secretary: Donald Morse.

> This society is composed of college and university faculty members interested in furthering knowledge of teaching and in presenting new research about English literature and other associated subjects in the humanities. There are numerous

regional groups of this organization that hold local meetings for discussion and for the reading of research papers, and there is a society-sponsored annual convention. The society publishes the **CEA Critic, CEA Forum**, and local newsletters.

Modern Humanities Research Association (MHRA). George Washington University, D.C. 20006. American secretary: Calvin Linton.

An organization of teachers and scholars of English and of other modern European languages and literature, MHRA seeks to provide impetus to research and the exchange of information in its field. It offers many useful publications, including the **Annual Bibliography of English Language and Literature, The Year's Work in Modern Language Studies**, and **Modern Language Review**. This organization has its headquarters in England, but has numerous American members.

Modern Language Association of America (MLA). 62 Fifth Avenue, New York, N.Y. 10011.

This is a prestigious organization composed of college and university teachers of English and other modern foreign languages. This society, vitally interested in linguistics as well as literature, works to improve teaching methods as well as to encourage research. Numerous publications emanating from the MLA are basic and indispensable to English students, teachers, and scholars. Among these publications are the **MLA International Bibliography**, the **MLA Abstracts**, and, of course, the society's journal **PMLA**. There are also other valuable research studies, books, pamphlets, and reports, as well as an annual directory of members. Words really are not adequate to describe the importance of this group and its publications; **PMLA** and allied materials are fundamental for all English students.

National Council of Teachers of English (NCTE). 1111 Kenyon Road, Urbana, Ill. 61801.

NCTE membership is open to teachers of English at all levels (elementary, secondary, college, and university). An extremely large and active organization, NCTE is designed to give information on teaching methods and techniques, and to increase awareness of new developments and research in the field. It publishes **College English, English Journal**, and numerous other books, pamphlets, and recordings, and also makes film strips available. It sponsors the Conference on College Composition and Communication, regional meetings, and holds an annual convention.

24. *Nonprint Information Sources*

In recent years audiovisual and nonprint materials have increased in volume and importance. Many such materials are used in classrooms, and more and more they have found their way into library and research use. The terms "audiovisual" and "nonprint" usually refer to the following types of materials, or media: (1) sound recordings; (2) films, filmstrips, and slides; (3) television cassettes; (4) microform; (5) programmed instruction materials; and (6) machine-readable texts.

Many colleges and universities have separate facilities for nonprint resources, while other institutions incorporate them into their regular library holdings. In attempting to search a library's resources for these materials one must, of course, determine whether they are listed separately or are included in the main card catalog.

At present there is no single definitive guide to audiovisual material. Therefore the practice in many libraries is to retain publishers' and producers' catalogs and use them for reference. A printed guide to these catalogs is the Bowker **Index**, cited below.

Index to Instructional Media Catalogs. New York: Bowker, 1974.

> This volume indexes more than six hundred hardware and software producers by both subject/media and product/services.

Perhaps the best available general guides to nonprint media are the indexes published by the National Information Center for Educational Media (University of Southern California, University Park, Los Angeles, Calif. 90007). These include the indexes listed below.

Index to 16mm Educational Films (2 Vol). [70,000 entries]

Index to 35mm Filmstrips (2 Vol.). [42,000 entries]

Index to Educational Audio Tapes. [20,000 entries]

Index to Educational Records. [18,000 entries]

Index to 8mm Motion Cartridges. [18,000 entries]

Index to Educational Overhead Transparencies. [35,000 entries]

Other useful guides on media reviews and resources in English are the three following.

Multi-Media Reviews Index. Edward C. Wall and B. Penny Northern, compilers. Ann Arbor: Pierian Press. [Annually; quarterly supplements]

International Index to Multi-Media Information 1970-1972. New York: Audio-Visual Associates/Bowker, 1975.

NCTE Resources for English and the Language Arts. National Council of Teachers of English, 1111 Kenyon Road, Urbana, Illinois 61801. [Annually]

SOUND RECORDINGS

Most libraries maintain collections of sound recordings, some of them running into the thousands. Usually these collections include both discs and cassettes, with cassettes becoming increasingly popular.

Recordings of poets reading from their own works are probably the most commonly encountered audiovisual resource in the field of literature. Poetry is written primarily to be heard and listening to a poet can provide unique insights. However, one should not overlook records and tapes of readings by others; sometimes they are superior to the poet's own renditions.

In addition, there are many recorded versions of major dramatic works that are well worth listening to for interpretations by renowned actors or directors. Recordings in Old English can be invaluable in learning to appreciate and master this all but foreign language. Speeches, scholarly criticism, and innumerable other types of works have been given new life and value through sound recordings increasingly available on cassette tapes.

One of the many publishers' cassette catalogs is that of Everett/Edwards, Inc. (P.O. Box 1060, Deland, Florida 32720), which lists available cassettes about poetry, drama, novels, world literature, and additional subjects, such as writing a research paper, of interest to English students. These cassettes feature prominent scholars who have recorded literary criticism, analyses, and interpretations of a vast number of authors, subjects, and literary movements. Jeffrey Norton Publishers, Inc. (145 East 49th Street, New York, N.Y. 10017) is another example of a company which prints its own catalog, listing many tapes and other recorded materials. In addition to a considerable number of literary critiques, Jeffrey Norton Publishers has available the Sound Seminar collection which includes the YM-YWHA Poetry Center Series of live recordings of contemporary poets, writers, and critics. Caedmon Records (505 Eighth Avenue, New York, N.Y. 10018) and Spoken Arts (310 North Avenue, New Rochelle, N.Y. 10801) offer an impressive number of phonograph records of authors reading from their own works or reading the writings of others. A large collection of literary cassettes is also available from the Center for Cassette Studies (8110 Webb Avenue, North Hollywood, Calif. 91605).

MICROFORM

"Microform" is the generic term used to refer to any or all of the following.

Microfilm contains page images that are usually reduced 15 to 24 times. Images may be positive or negative. The film is usually 35 or 16mm and may contain several thousand page images on reels or in cartridges.

Microfiche is 4⅛ x 5¾-inch film "card," or "fiche," containing page images that are reduced 15 to 200 times. Federal standards now call for a reduction ratio of 24:1, which allows 98 ordinary-size pages per fiche. Images may be positive or negative.

Microprint refers to material **printed** on paper in sizes that are reduced 10 to 25 times. The images are therefore always positive. Microprint is available in card forms that range in size from 3 x 5 to 8½ x 11 inches.

All microforms require a viewer to display images in a readable size. Microform reader/printers permit making paper copies of displayed images—an extremely important feature for the researcher.

Vast collections of literary works are available in microform, numbering in the millions of volumes. Many of these volumes would not be available to most scholars if it were not for microform. The new **Dictionary of Old English** could not have been undertaken by computer unless over five hundred Old English manuscripts had first been microfilmed and collected at one central university location. Many rare and important works are now available for the first time to students in the United States; for example, there is University Microfilms' project of microfilming all titles in Pollard and Redgrave's **Short-Title Catalogue of Books Printed in England, Scotland and Ireland . . . 1475-1640**. Readex has made many sixteenth- and seventeenth-century plays obtainable. These are facsimiles, of course, but most colleges and universities have few, if any, of these works, and those that they do have are in the library's rare book room only.

Three invaluable reference works about microforms are now available in most libraries, and each guide performs an indispensable service.

Guide to Microfilms in Print. Washington, D.C.: Microcard Editions, Inc., 1961-   [Annually]

> This publication is arranged in alphabetical order and indicates the books, journals, and similar materials available on microfilm or on other microforms. Books are recorded by author while periodicals and sets are listed by title. Newspapers are entered by state and city. The names and addresses of the publishers are recorded as well as the price of each item. Also provided is the form in which the material is available, that is, on microfilm, opaque copies, or microfiche. Theses and dissertations are omitted, probably because they are adequately recorded by **Dissertation Abstracts International**. Although the **Guide** is the best record available, it is not complete. American micropublishers are invited to list their offerings; therefore the materials of those who decline, as well as those of European publishers, do not appear.

National Register of Microform Masters. Washington, D.C.: Library of Congress, 1965-   [Annually]

> This reference work is designed to record all important available microfilm masters from which libraries may acquire prints if they so desire. This **National Register** is not intended to supply master microfilms to readers but rather to identify the location of these materials so copies may be requested.

Subject Guide to Microforms in Print. Washington, D.C.: Microcard Editions, Inc., 1966-   [Biennially]

> This valuable guide lists those microfilm, microcard, microprint, and microfiche materials which are obtainable from publishers and suppliers in the United States. Books are listed by author, while journals and sets are recorded by title. Newspapers are arranged by states. Complete addresses of publishers are given so that an individual or library may contact the publisher and quickly obtain the particular title he wishes in the form in which it is available.

PROGRAMMED INSTRUCTION MATERIALS

Much carefully structured learning material has been developed according to the teaching-machine concepts originally formulated by the psychologist B. F. Skinner. These programmed learning materials are available in various media including print, film, and computer-based files. Many have been developed for instruction in English. The following are helpful guides to what is available.

Programmed Instruction Guide. 3 vols. Newburyport, Mass.: Entelek, Inc. (42 Pleasant Street).

Programmed Learning, and Individually Paced Instruction Biography. Bay City, Mich.: Hendershot Programmed Learning (4114 Ridgwood Drive).

MACHINE-READABLE TEXTS

A marriage between the computer and literary research is not as improbable as it might appear. The full texts of many literary works have been input to the computer and are now available for machine textual and linguistic analyses.

One of the most common by-products of the computerization of literary materials is the concordance, which is an alphabetically arranged listing, in context, of all uses of all words appearing in a given work or works (see Chapter 22). Concordances have been produced for many major literary works and are available in printed form. A partial listing of published concordances can be found in **Books in Print** and in the indexes of the sources listed below. The two journals are major sources of information on computer-based literary material. The directory, as indicated, is also useful.

Computers and the Humanities. Elmsford, N.Y.: Pergamon. [Bimonthly]

> Joseph Raben, the editor of this journal, was a pioneering scholar in the field and is today one of its leaders. The journal publishes an annual bibliography of computer/humanities research.

ALLC Bulletin (Bulletin of the Association for Literary and Linguistic Computing). [Triannually]

> Joan M. Smith is editor of this bulletin. Its editorial offices are 6 Seven Oaks Avenue, Heaton Moor, Stockport, Chesire, SK 4 4AW, England.

Computer-oriented Research in the Humanities: A Directory of Scholars Active. Elmsford, N.Y.: Pergamon.

> This new directory is particularly useful because its index lists computer research by subject.

An Afterword Leading Forward

The study of literature can be an ongoing adventure, reaching far beyond the books and journals mentioned here. At times, thoughtful reading will provide information and suggestions that will lead to further sources not immediately apparent. One student, for example, after reading several of Willa Cather's novels, wondered about Cather's spiritual beliefs and consulted the standard biographies. After much additional reading the student discovered that Miss Cather had an unmarried sister who at that time was still living. Further investigation resulted in the student's obtaining the sister's address, and a correspondence followed. From this interchange, the student learned much more than any book had yet told of Willa Cather's humanitarian concerns and her membership in the Episcopal church. Imagine the student's feelings when she used this heretofore unknown information in a research paper, and imagine the professor's feelings when he read it!

Living authors will sometimes answer queries, thereby solving certain research problems that no standard references can solve. The authors may be asked about specific influences on their books and thoughts, or about particular textual matters or allusions, or about their precise views of some character or event.

One never knows just where or when new information may turn up, as is shown by the well-known case of James Boswell's journals and other papers. When in 1920 Chauncey B. Tinker, a Yale professor, wrote to the London **Times** seeking information about the possible existence of Boswell letters, he received an anonymous reply, "Try Malahide Castle." At this estate near Dublin, Tinker was allowed to view some of Boswell's letters, diaries, and manuscript pages of his **Life of Samuel Johnson**. He was also told by Boswell's descendants that there were other materials which had been put in storage. Eventually, in 1928, an American collector named Colonel Ralph Isham was able to purchase these papers. In subsequent years other Boswell manuscripts were found in a croquet box and in an old stable at Malahide.

Meanwhile, Professor Claude Abbott was looking for materials about James Beattie, a minor eighteenth-century writer. His search took him to Fettercairn House, a large estate in Scotland. There many more letters and manuscripts relating to Boswell, Johnson, and others were discovered. After long negotiations these papers came into the possession of Colonel Isham and now rest at Yale University Library. As a result of these happenings, many of Boswell's diaries and papers have been printed in recent years, and a whole new light has been shed on the man, on his literary acquaintances, and on the era in which he wrote.

Some individuals regard the Boswell treasure trove as unique; and indeed, on the basis of total amount of discovered material, this may be true. But new discoveries, albeit on a lesser scale, are constantly being made. In a house that was recently being dismantled in Wilkes-Barre, Pennsylvania, a weatherworn tome was found in the attic. It turned out to be the original handwritten manuscript of one of Washington Irving's books. A diary by Irving (one he kept while he was in Spain and heretofore not even known to exist) turned up in a house in Westbury, Long Island.

Such finds are by no means uncommon. One student searching for a thesis topic found his material by coming upon a dilapidated volume in a dustworn secondhand bookstore. Perusal of the book revealed that the author, who had been fairly well known in his own time, had written analyses of Alexander Pope's translations of Homer's **Iliad** and **Odyssey**, two of the most famous literary translations ever produced. In the course of further studying the student found a statement by Thomas De Quincey, who claimed that he had a trunkful of the critic's manuscripts. So far, these materials have not been found, but it is not impossible that they will be, eventually.

There are all kinds of missing literary materials. Herman Melville's letters to Nathaniel Hawthorne, for instance, may someday come to light. Forty diaries of William Cullen Bryant's mother are believed to be in existence, but their present location is still a mystery. The important thing is to be alert, to think of such possibilities, to be grounded in the fundamentals, to examine books and references carefully, and to seek further leads. If this present book better prepares its readers by furnishing knowledge of the basic sources in the field of English studies, it will have more than adequately accomplished its purpose.

Index

This index gives primarily *names* and *titles*. For particular periods and types of literature, as well as the nationalities covered, see the Table of Contents.